fresh felt
FLOWERS

17 STUNNING FLOWERS TO SEW & DISPLAY

LYNNE FARRIS

C&T PUBLISHING

Text © 2007 Lynne Farris

Artwork © 2007 C&T Publishing, Inc.

Publisher: Amy Marson

Editorial Director: Gailen Runge

Acquisitions Editor: Jan Grigsby

Editor: Lynn Koolish

Technical Editors: Teresa Stroin and Nanette Zeller

Copyeditor/Proofreader: Wordfirm Inc.

Cover Designer/Book Designer: Kristy K. Zacharias

Illustrator: Richard Sheppard

Production Coordinator: Tim Manibusan

Photography by C&T Publishing, Inc., unless otherwise noted

Locations and photo styling: Diane Pedersen and Lynn Koolish

Props: Lynn Koolish, Diane Pedersen, Ruth Koolish, and Sheila Pedersen

Published by C&T Publishing, Inc., P.O. Box 1456, Lafayette, CA 94549

Library of Congress Cataloging-in-Publication Data

Farris, Lynne.

  Fresh felt flowers : 17 stunning flowers to sew & display / Lynne Farris.

    p. cm.

  ISBN-13: 978-1-57120-415-8 (paper trade : alk. paper)

  ISBN-10: 1-57120-415-6 (paper trade : alk. paper)

  1. Fabric flowers. 2. Machine sewing. 3. Felt work. I. Title.

  TT890.5.F37 2007

  746--dc22

  2006035952

Printed in China

10 9 8 7 6 5 4 3 2 1

dedication

For almost twenty years, my friend Mary Woodall and I have fearlessly explored the outer limits of our imagination while sharing our love of sewing. Through trial and many hilarious errors, we've figured out how to turn fabric into just about everything, from giant costumed characters and a whale golf cart to the beautifully refined sculpted felt flowers contained in this book. Like Lucy and Ethel, we've schemed and dreamed, laughed uproariously, and somehow managed to amaze even ourselves with what we have been able to create together. This book is a testament to the gift of creative collaboration. Thanks, Mary!

acknowledgments

Thanks to Gailen Runge, Amy Marson, Jan Grigsby, and all the wonderful people at C&T Publishing who gave me this opportunity, and especially to Lynn Koolish, my editor, for patiently pulling this book out of me, practically word by word; Teresa Stroin, for carefully checking on all the details I would have so easily overlooked; and Diane Pedersen, for her beautiful and artful photography that brings each flower to life on the page. Many thanks to Lambert Greene, who always supports my creative work and gets it to FedEx just before they lock the doors, and to Gabrielle Kinge, my studio assistant, for cheerfully helping with whatever needs to be done.

blooming houseplants

perennial favorites

exotic tropicals

Introduction 5

Tools and Materials 6

Basic Techniques 8

Blooming Houseplants

    African Violet 12

    Gerbera Daisy 15

    Geranium 20

    Tulip 24

    Daffodil 29

    Nasturtium 33

Perennial Favorites

    Calla Lily 36

    Rose 39

    Sunflower 43

    Gladiolus 47

    Magnolia 52

    Iris 56

Exotic Tropicals

    Ginger 60

    Bird of Paradise 63

    Anthurium 67

    Heliconia 70

    Orchid Plant 74

About the Author 79

Resources 79

introduction

I come from a long line of garden enthusiasts with whom I have shared a lifelong fascination with flowers and plants. The infinite combinations of color, texture, shape, and botanical forms are an endless source of inspiration for me as I seek to re-create and celebrate Mother Nature's boundless beauty.

My other passion in life is fabric, and I have been quite fortunate to have turned my passion into a very satisfying profession. I've crafted a career in sculpting with fabric to design and make toys, puppets, props for commercials, costumes, and various home décor items. Each design project taught me more and more about the potential of materials and how to make just about anything I want out of fabric.

This book is the culmination of all those years of fabric-sculpting experience coupled with my love of nature. From the simplest African Violet to the most exotically blooming Bird of Paradise, you're sure to find some plants and flowers within these pages that will inspire you. Furthermore, you'll be delighted to know that even though they look complex enough to impress your friends mightily, they are actually easy to make, requiring no more than simple stitching on the machine and a hot glue gun.

Recently, I've discovered the joy of fabric sculpting with wool felt. It comes in an amazing array of colors and is sturdy and sculptable. It is delightfully easy to work with because it cuts cleanly and doesn't fray, eliminating the need for turning seams—every step of the process is simplified.

The real beauty secret of these designs lies in joining together layers of felt by topstitching, creating texture and visual interest while strengthening the fabrics so that they can practically stand alone.

Whether you are a beginner or an accomplished sewer, you'll find that you can easily achieve success making these delightful fabric sculptures. The book contains projects for every style, taste, and skill level, with complete patterns and easy-to-follow instructions.

It's important that you read through the chapter on basic techniques before you embark on this creative adventure. You'll find that some things seem a little backward at first, such as stitching first, **then** cutting out, but once you try this approach you'll see just how easy it is to achieve spectacular results.

Felt flowers make wonderful seasonal accents for your home and much-appreciated gifts for friends and family. Enjoy!

&tools
MATERIALS

wool felt

All the projects in this book were created with wool felt as the fabric. Wool felt is available in a variety of blends and weights that offer great options when sculpting flowers. Check your local quilt shop or fabric store, or see Resources on page 79.

For the sturdiest of petals and leaves, 100% wool felt offers the most body. You can layer as necessary to create the thickness and firmness you need. You will find that top-stitching the layers together adds strength and stability while offering unlimited opportunity for embellishment. The more stitching you add, the stiffer the fabric becomes. Some of the wool/rayon blends offer the added option of washing them to create a dimpled surface that mimics textures found in nature.

stems

Floral stems are available in several lengths and thicknesses for the various styles of flowers. In addition, you can add flexible plastic tubing that fits over the floral stems to add dimension or to join several small stems together into a larger branch. The floral stems that are specified in the projects are available online (see Resources, page 79). You can also check your local craft or floral supply store for similar stems, and your local hardware or home improvement store for a variety of wire and flexible tubing.

Covered florist wire is called for in many projects for use as a stem or to add support inside a petal or leaf. Use 18-gauge wire for small stems and for supporting larger leaves. For small petals, thinner and more flexible 26-gauge wire adds sufficient strength.

beading wire

Some of the flower centers require threading beads onto colored wire and twisting them to create stamens. Anodized beading wire is available in a full palette of colors to coordinate with your beads and flowers. For these applications, 28-gauge wire is sufficiently strong.

Use anodized beading wire to make beaded stamens.

Wool felt

marking tools

Marking on felt is fairly simple and ensures the accuracy of your stitching lines. Since you will be stitching directly onto the lines, avoid using pencils or permanent ink that will leave unsightly marks on your project. Instead, use an air- or water-soluble fabric marker for marking outlines on lighter colors and a chalk wheel or chalk pencil for marking on darker colors.

Use air- or water-soluble marker or chalk for marking on fabric.

cutting tools

Sharp-pointed scissors and a rotary cutter and cutting mat are essential for accurately cutting out sewn shapes. Additionally, some projects call for a scallop- or pinking-edge rotary blade to give a ruffled edge. To cut smoothly using scissors, hold your scissors still while guiding the fabric through the blades.

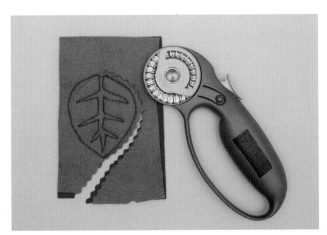

Use scallop-edge rotary blade for ruffled edge.

glue gun and clips

A trigger-feed hot glue gun is essential when assembling flowers and plants. To apply glue into small areas, place a drop of hot glue on a nonporous surface such as glass, and immediately use a straight pin to apply a small amount of glue where needed. Hold the glue joint tightly until it is completely cool to ensure a good bond. Use clothespins or clips to hold the pieces together while the glue cures. When cool, excess glue can be clipped away with small scissors.

Use clips to hold glued pieces together while curing.

sewing machine

Your sewing machine is the key tool for ensuring the success of these projects. You will need a straight stitch and a zigzag stitch. An open-toe embroidery foot is helpful if you have one because it makes it easier to see your marked lines for stitching. If you want to free-motion stitch, you'll need to be able to lower the feed dogs and you'll need a free-motion embroidery foot.

Do yourself a favor and have your machine serviced and treat yourself to a new needle before embarking on a new project. You will find that felt creates a fair amount of lint, so clean out the race and presser-foot assembly regularly to ensure smooth operation.

basic
TECHNIQUES

The stitching and cutting techniques used for most of these projects, while quite simple, may seem somewhat unfamiliar if you have been accustomed to quilting or fashion sewing. Read this chapter thoroughly before starting on any of the projects, and you will be able to achieve dazzling success with a minimum of effort. You can also use these techniques to create your own designs for your favorite flowers and plants.

using templates and patterns

The pattern templates located on the pullout pages at the back of the book should be traced onto tracing paper—transfer all the stitching lines. Adhere the traced patterns with fusible web or spray adhesive to a firm cardstock for ease in tracing shapes onto the felt. Unless otherwise indicated, the outline of the pattern template is the outermost stitching line and therefore the exact shape of the finished piece. Since you will be making these flowers from felt, you won't need any seam allowances for turning seams. You will be cutting out the pieces just beyond the stitching lines, so leave margins of about $1/4$″ between pieces as you trace. Trace the pattern templates directly onto the right side of the felt using an air-soluble marker for light colors or a chalk marker for darker colors.

Trace around pattern templates.

transferring topstitching lines

To transfer the topstitching lines from the pattern template to the fabric, use a large embroidery needle or a stylus to punch holes in the templates along the topstitching lines. Then use an air- or water-soluble marker to mark the dots and connect them to form the topstitching lines. You might find that after a few times you won't need to connect the dots and you can just use the dots as your guide for topstitching.

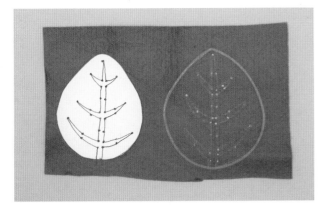

Connect dots to form topstitching lines.

interlocking pattern layout

When transferring patterns to fabric, it is sometimes possible to lay out the templates in an interlocking pattern so that when they are sewn and cut apart, one cut yields two usable edges.

You can often use two parallel rows of stitching with about $1/4''$ between them to create this effect. This is especially useful when making several of the same flower.

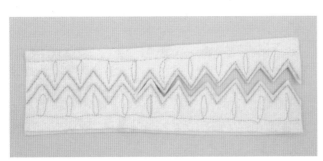

Interlocking pattern layout

layering the felt

Some patterns call for two layers of felt, either in contrasting colors or of the same color to create a firmer or fleshier flower part.

You can pin them together if you want to, but I usually find it unnecessary. Once you use your hands to smooth over the two layers to remove any puckers or wrinkles, the layers will cling together quite easily. You'll find that very little shifting takes place once you begin to stitch the layers together. If you do decide to pin the layers together, pin around the outer edges of the fabric, not inside the traced shapes, to avoid distorting the shapes of the petals and leaves by sewing over the pins.

stitch, THEN cut

You will find it helpful to trace all the pieces at once, layering the felt together as indicated in the instructions. Then stitch along all the outlines, and do any topstitching required **before** cutting out the sewn shapes. This simplifies stitching and shortens your cutting time. You will also find that it is easier to move the fabric under the needle of the sewing machine before cutting the shapes out, because you have something to hold onto as you guide the fabric.

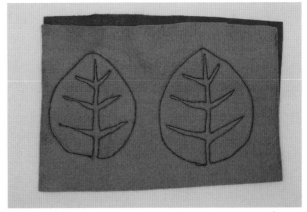

*Stitch **before** cutting.*

topstitching

Use contrasting thread when topstitching to add visual interest. When sewing two contrasting layers of felt together, you can match the bobbin thread to the upper fabric and the upper thread to the fabric underneath for a contrasting but coordinated look. For best results, check your upper thread and bobbin tension by stitching on a scrap of the double fabrics to be sure that the contrasting threads aren't pulling through to the other side.

To create the topstitching on petals and leaves, it is often easiest to use a free-motion embroidery foot and lower the feed dogs on your machine so that you can move the fabric about freely under the needle. You can then draw with the thread, stitching along the topstitching lines to create intricate patterns and textures as you stitch. If you are new to free-motion stitching, this is a great way to try it out. The most important thing to know is that the length of your stitch is determined by how fast you move the fabric in relation to how fast the needle is going up and down, so my best advice is to move the fabric slowly while holding the foot pedal down at a steady speed. You'll create small, fairly evenly spaced stitches and will have more control over where they end up—always a good thing!

If you prefer, the stitching can be done with the feed dogs up, if you stitch carefully and pivot as often as needed to get smooth curves.

Topstitching

flat-joining seams

To join two pieces of felt together without adding the bulk of a regular seam and seam allowance, set the machine to a narrow zigzag stitch. Put an open-toe embroidery foot on your machine, butt the edges of the felt together, and center them under the presser foot. Stitch carefully, using matching thread, and adjust the edges while stitching to accommodate any curves. This is a great way to create a natural-looking dimensional petal or leaf.

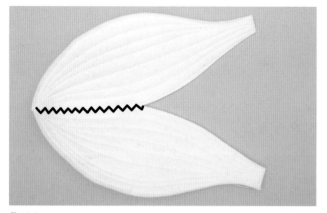

Flat-join seam.

wrapping and layering

Some of the flowers seem complex because they are made up of numerous layers of duplicate small pieces. A great way to simplify putting all those pieces together is to stitch a continuous strip of repetitive shapes, then either wrap and glue them around a stem or roll the strip itself to form the layers. Glue along the straight edge and attach the layers together so that each layer covers the glue of the previous one.

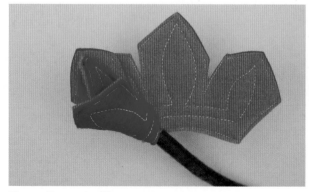

Wrap and layer to simplify construction.

stitch and flip

This technique allows you to sculpt a flower or petal, adding dimension and revealing a contrasting fabric from the back side. First topstitch the piece as indicated, then cut it out and fold as instructed. Stitch across the folded piece where indicated and then turn it inside out along that seam to create a multilayered dimensional form.

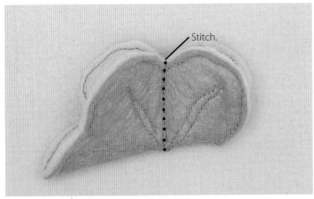

Stitch across folded piece.

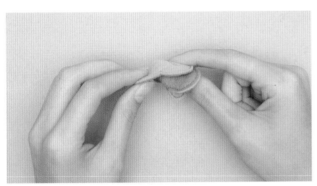

Turn inside out along seam.

Dimensional form

stem covers

Each project will specify a certain diameter and length of stem and the amount of felt required to cover it. To sew the stem covers, fold the felt stem cover lengthwise around the stem. Measure and mark along the full length to create a snug fit. Some flowers specify tapering the stem cover outward to a wider width at one end to accommodate the flower back or to slide over wires connecting the flower to the stem.

Sew the stem cover along the marked line, then slide it onto the stem **before cutting away the seam allowance** to be sure that it fits snugly. Remove the cover from the stem, and use a rotary cutter to cut away excess fabric close to the stitching. Slide the stem cover over the stem again, and fold and glue the ends of the cover neatly over one end of the stem. Consult the instructions for the individual project for attaching the other end of the stem to the flower or leaf.

Insert stem and glue closed.

fringe

Some of the flower centers call for a purchased faux suede fringe (see Resources, page 79.) If you prefer to make your own fringe, cut a 1″ × 24″ strip of creamy yellow felt using a clear ruler and rotary cutter.

Align the ruler along the length of the strip, $1/4$″ from the edge. Hold it firmly in place, and use the markings on the ruler as your guide to make perpendicular cuts at $1/8$″ intervals along the entire length of the strip. Use the ruler as your stop in order to create uniform cuts.

A small pot of delicate African Violets sitting on the kitchen windowsill brings back a flood of nostalgic memories of my grand-mother's kitchen.

Re-created here in wool felt, this charming houseplant forms a nosegay of leaves surrounding the cluster of blooms.

If you prefer, you can group one flower with three small leaves in a teacup, fill the cup with small pebbles, and place it on a matching saucer for a hostess gift that's sure to delight.

African Violet

materials

See pages 6–7 for basic supplies.

TO MAKE THE PLANT AS SHOWN, YOU WILL NEED:

DARK PURPLE FELT: 1 piece 4″ × 7″ for the petals

LIGHT PURPLE FELT: 1 piece 5″ × 8″ for the petals

LEAF GREEN FELT: 1 piece 11″ × 17″ for the leaves; scraps for the flower backs

CRANBERRY FELT: 1 piece 11″ × 17″ for the leaves

26-GAUGE FLORIST WIRE: 5 pieces, each 15″ long, for the flowers

18-GAUGE COVERED FLORIST WIRE: 13 pieces, each 9″ long, for the leaves

YELLOW GLASS E-BEADS: 10 for the flower centers

FLORIST TAPE

instructions

See pages 8–11 for basic techniques.

Make the Petals and Leaves

1. Make templates for the African Violet 2- and 3-petal pieces; the small, medium, and large leaves; and the flower back using the patterns on the pullout.

2. Trace the 2-petal template 5 times (once for each flower) onto dark purple felt. Trace the 3-petal template 5 times (once for each flower) onto light purple felt. Transfer the topstitching lines.

3. Trace the small and large leaf templates 5 times each, and the medium leaf template 3 times onto leaf green felt. Transfer the topstitching lines. Layer this marked felt with a piece of cranberry felt.

4. **Before cutting out each piece,** stitch carefully around the outlines. Use coordinating thread for the flower petals and contrasting thread for the leaves. Topstitch as indicated to create surface texture on the flower petals and veins on the leaves. When topstitching the leaves, be sure to leave the center channels open at the bases of the leaves for inserting the wire.

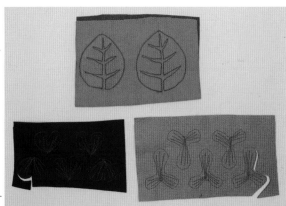

*Stitch leaves and petals **before** cutting.*

5. Cut out the flower petals slightly beyond the outline stitching using scissors, clipping close to the stitching at inside points.

6. Cut out the leaves slightly beyond the outline stitching using a pinking-blade rotary cutter to create the decorative edge.

7. Insert the 18-gauge covered florist wire through the channel in each leaf, leaving about 6″–8″ of wire extending as a stem from each leaf. Use a tiny drop of hot glue to secure the wire to the leaf at the base.

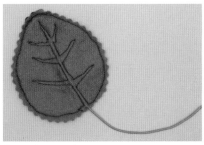

Cut out leaves and insert wire.

Make the Flowers

1. Arrange a 2-petal piece so that the point is centered over a 3-petal piece as shown.

Arrange African Violet pieces.

2. Pull the long petal firmly through the center between the 2 dark petals and fold it flat, as shown.

Pull long petal through center.

3. Fold the flower in half lengthwise, matching dark petals to dark and light petals to light.

4. Thread 2 yellow glass E-beads onto a length of 26-gauge wire and thread the wire through the center of the folded flower between the petals.

Fold lengthwise.

5. Use a pair of pliers to twist the wire tightly on the under-side of the flower, making certain that the beads are at the center front of the flower.

Thread wire through center of folded flower between petals and twist together.

6. Open the flowers and shape the petals to form small cuplike shapes.

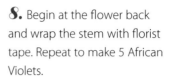

Open flower and shape petals.

7. Cut out the flower backs from a single layer of scrap green felt. Cut a small slit in the center of the flower back and slip it onto the wire, gluing it in place on the back of the flower with a small drop of hot glue.

Add flower backs.

8. Begin at the flower back and wrap the stem with florist tape. Repeat to make 5 African Violets.

Wrap stem.

Put the Plant Together

1. Gather together the 5 African Violets so that they form a cluster.

2. Arrange the 5 small leaves closely around the flowers.

3. Add the 3 medium leaves, spacing them evenly under the small leaves.

4. Add the 5 largest leaves, spacing them evenly around the medium leaves and shaping the wires in the leaves so that they point slightly downward.

5. Twist the wires together and wrap with florist tape to secure.

Arrange leaves around flowers and wrap wires with florist tape.

6. Use the photograph of the finished flowers (page 12) as a guide to shape and arrange the petals and leaves to simulate authentic blooms.

This perky little Gerbera Daisy plant is the perfect accent to brighten up a bare corner or grace a sunny windowsill. It goes together quite easily, with a minimum of effort, so you might keep several on hand for last-minute birthday or get-well gifts for friends or family members.

Live Gerbera Daisies grow in a full palette of colors, so you can expand your color options to include a variety of shades from creamy whites to yellows, oranges, pinks, and reds. The lighter ones tend to have dark centers and the darker ones, light centers—take a bit of artistic license if you like. I'm sure Mother Nature will approve of your creativity.

Gerbera Daisy

materials

See pages 6–7 for basic supplies.

TO MAKE THE PLANT AS SHOWN, YOU WILL NEED:

CRANBERRY FELT: 2 pieces, each 5″ × 10″, for the petals

YELLOW-ORANGE FELT: 1 circle, 1^1/$_2$″ in diameter, cut with a scallop-edge rotary cutter for the flower center

LEAF GREEN FELT: 2 pieces, each 16″ × 20″, for the leaves; 2 pieces, each 3″ × 3″, for the flower back; 1 strip 1^1/$_2$″ × 17″ for the flower stem cover

1″-WIDE CREAMY YELLOW FAUX SUEDE FRINGE: ^{2}/$_3$ yard (I use Wright's. See Resources, page 79, or page 11 to make your own.)

^{1}/$_4$″-DIAMETER STEM: 1 piece 15″ long

18-GAUGE COVERED FLORIST WIRE: 7 pieces, each 10″ long, for the leaves

FLORIST TAPE

instructions

See pages 8–11 for basic techniques.

Make the Flower

1. Make templates for the Gerbera Daisy petals, flower center, flower back, and leaf using the patterns on the pullout.

2. Trace the circle flower template twice onto one piece of cranberry felt. To easily mark the topstitching lines, mark the center of the circle and the dots around the outer edge, then use a ruler to connect the dots to the center mark. Layer this marked felt with the other piece of cranberry felt.

3. **Before cutting out the flower,** topstitch using contrasting thread, beginning and ending about ^{1}/$_2$″ from the outer edge at each dot and passing through the exact center of the circle. Then cut out the circle along the outer edge using a scallop-edge rotary cutter.

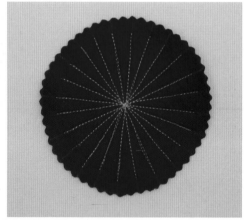

Stitch flowers, then cut out.

4. Use a regular rotary cutter to cut between the stitching lines from the outer edge to ^{1}/$_2$″ from the center to create petals. Trim the outer points from each petal to shape.

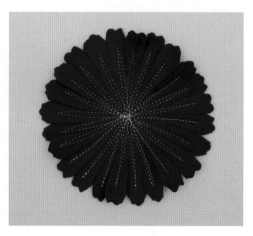

Cut between stitching lines and trim away points from each petal.

5. Repeat the process to create a second layer of petals.

6. Stack the layers of petals, matching the edges. Arrange the yellow-orange circle over the center. Stitch through all the layers, 1/4″ in from the outer edge of the yellow-orange circle, to secure them.

Stitch through all layers to secure.

7. To make the center pom-pom, use a rotary cutter and straightedge to trim 2/3 yard of fringe gradually from 1/2″ at one end to full width at the other end.

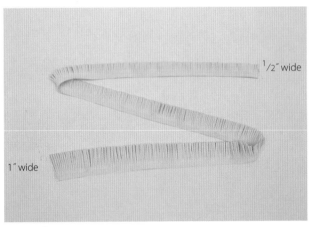

Trimmed fringe

8. Begin rolling and wrapping the fringe from the narrowest end. Wind tightly until all the fringe is wound into a pom-pom, and the fringe radiates from the center toward the outer edges in a regular pattern. Glue from the back to secure it. Hold it tightly until the glue is dry.

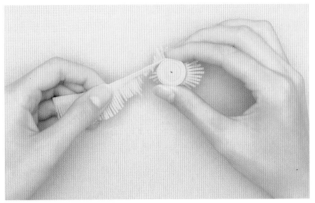

Wrap fringe to form pom-pom.

9. Apply glue to the back of the pom-pom and glue the pom-pom over the yellow circle in the center of the flower.

Glue pom-pom to center of flower.

Make the Stem and Flower Back

1. Fold the stem cover in half lengthwise. Measure and stitch it to create a snug fit for the stem. Trim the seam allowance close to the stitching. Slide the cover onto the stem and glue it closed at both ends.

2. Bend the stem at one end to form a loop perpendicular to the length of the stem. Glue the loop to the center back of the flower. Hold it in a vertical position until the glue is dry.

Glue bent stem to center back of flower.

3. To make the flower back, trace the template onto leaf green felt. Layer this marked felt with another layer of leaf green felt. Stitch all around and on both sides of the slit line using coordinating thread.

Stitch along outline and on both sides of slit line.

4. Cut out the flower back slightly beyond the stitching using a scallop-edge rotary cutter, and slit along the slit line with scissors or a straight-edge cutter.

5. Arrange the flower back created in Step 4 over the stem loop that is attached to the back of the flower, and glue it in place, overlapping the edges to fit snugly.

Glue flower back over stem loop.

Make the Leaves

1. Trace the leaf template 7 times onto leaf green felt. Transfer all the markings for the topstitching and wire channel. Layer this marked felt with another layer of leaf green felt.

2. Stitch all around the outside edges using coordinating thread, leaving an opening at the lower edge of each leaf for inserting the wire.

3. Stitch a channel for the wire through the center of each leaf. Add topstitching to create veins and texture on the leaves. Cut out slightly beyond the outline stitching of the leaves.

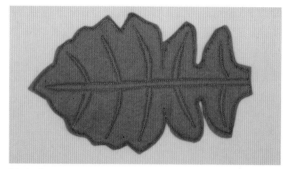

Stitch, then cut out.

4. Insert the covered florist wire through the channel in each leaf so that the wire extends about 3″ from the bottom of the leaf. Make a ¹/₂″ slit in one layer of the wire channel in each leaf and apply glue to secure the wire.

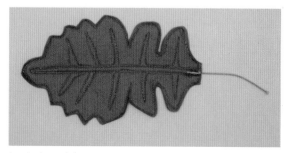

Insert wire and glue to secure.

5. Apply more glue along the lower edge of that same side of each leaf and pinch the leaf together as shown to create dimension. Use a clothespin or clip to hold the glued edges together while the glue cools and bonds completely.

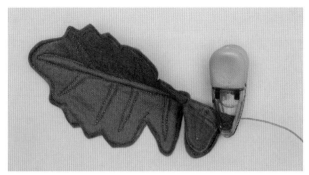

Pinch together edges to create dimension.

Put the Plant Together

1. Start about 5″ below the flower, and arrange 3 leaves around the stem. Wrap the leaves' florist wires securely around the flower stem. Use florist tape to hold the leaves in place along the stem.

2. Gather and arrange the remaining leaves, and repeat the process so that leaves are interspersed evenly between the leaves in the previous layer. Continue wrapping the florist wires neatly around the stem and cover them with florist tape so that the flower and leaves all appear to grow from one central stem.

Wrap leaf wires and stem with florist tape.

3. Use the photograph of the finished plant as a guide to shape and arrange the petals and leaves to simulate an authentic bloom.

This little potted Geranium is sure to bring a nostalgic smile to the face of any gardener. The clusters of pink flowers framed by round lacy leaves make me think of porches and picket fences, pink lemonade, and summertime picnics. Enjoy this old-fashioned favorite.

geranium

materials

See pages 6–7 for basic supplies.

TO MAKE THE PLANT AS SHOWN, YOU WILL NEED:

LIGHT PINK FELT: **1 piece 26″ × 6″ for the flowers**

ROSE PINK FELT: **1 piece 26″ × 6″ for the flowers**

LIGHT GREEN FELT: **1 piece 26″ × 36″ for the leaves; 3 strips, each 26″ × 2″, for the stem covers**

MEDIUM GREEN FELT: **1 piece 24″ × 10″ for the leaf centers and flower backs**

26-GAUGE COVERED FLORIST WIRE: **32 pieces, each 8″ long, for the flowerets and the leaves**

¼″-DIAMETER STEM: **3 pieces, each 15″ long**

FLORIST TAPE

instructions

See pages 8–11 for basic techniques.

Make the Flowers

1. Make templates for the Geranium flower; the small, medium, and large leaves; the small, medium, and large leaf centers; and the flower back using the patterns on the pullout.

2. Trace the flower template 15 times onto rose pink felt. Transfer the top-stitching lines. Layer this marked felt with the light pink felt.

3. **Before cutting out the flowers,** stitch carefully around the outlines, using coordinating thread, and topstitch as indicated to create surface texture on the Geranium flower petals. Cut out the flowers close to the stitching.

*Stitch petals **before** cutting.*

4. Fold a flower in half with the light pink to the inside, and stitch across the center of the folded flower. Grasp the flower between your thumb and forefinger and turn it inside out to reveal an individual Geranium floweret. Repeat with the remaining flowers.

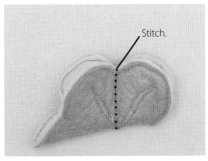

Fold flower and stitch.

Turn flower inside out.

Dimensional form of flower

5. Bend one end of an 8″ piece of wire into a crook about 1″ from the end. Apply glue to the crook and attach it at the seam on the underside of the flower so that the crook is at the center of the flower. Repeat with the remaining flowers.

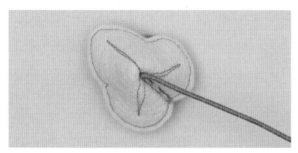

Glue florist wire onto flowers.

6. Trace 15 flower backs onto medium green felt. Cut out these pieces.

7. Cut a slit in one of the flower backs as drawn on the pattern. Thread the back onto the flower so that the slit fits over the crook in the wire and the opposite point is over the seam. Glue that point in place. Then grasp one of the other points and pull it to the opposite side and align it between the flower petals. Glue it in place. Pull the third point over the previous one; align and glue it between the opposite petals. Repeat with the remaining flowers.

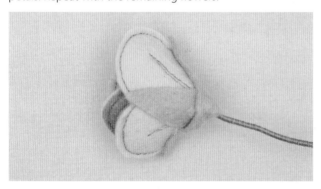

Attach flower backs to flowers.

Make the Leaves

1. Trace 7 small, 5 medium, and 5 large leaf centers onto medium green felt. Transfer the topstitching lines. Cut out these pieces and set them aside.

2. Trace 7 small, 5 medium, and 5 large leaves onto light green felt. Transfer the topstitching lines. Layer this marked felt with another piece of light green felt.

3. **Before cutting out the leaves,** stitch around the outlines of the leaves using coordinating thread, and arrange the leaf centers in place over the traced leaves. Topstitch to create the overall patterns of the veins and the wire channels on the leaves. Be sure to leave the center channel open at the base of each leaf and leaf center for inserting the wire.

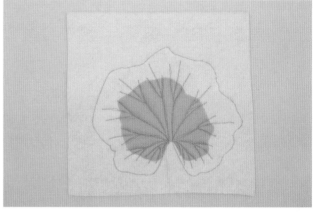

*Stitch leaves **before** cutting.*

4. Cut out the leaves using a scallop-edge rotary cutter. Insert wires into the channels. Cut a small slit on the underside of the leaf in the channel where the wire is inserted and apply glue to secure the wire.

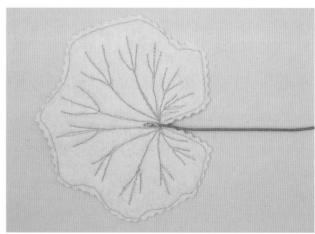

Cut slits in channels, and glue wires in place.

Make the Stems

1. Cut 12 lengths of stem cover 6″ long. Fold them in half lengthwise. Measure and stitch them to create a snug fit for the stems. Taper them outward close to the edge. Cut the seam allowance close to the stitching.

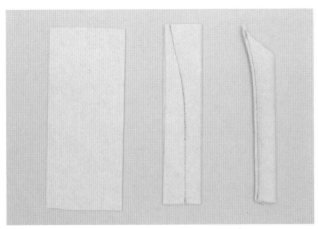

Sew stem covers.

Put the Plant Together

1. Gather together 6 flowers. Grasp the wires firmly together, and wrap them with florist tape. Align the taped wires with the flower stem, and wrap the wires and stem with tape to secure them. Slide a short stem cover over all the wires, and glue it together near the top to secure it.

2. Repeat with a second group of 6 flowers, and then with the last group of 3 flowers.

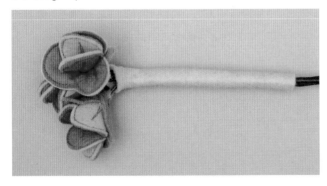

Align clusters of flowers with plant stem, wrap, and cover.

3. Gather together a cluster of small and medium leaves, arranged at random heights. Tape them together with florist tape. Align the taped wires to the flower stem, and wrap the wires with tape to secure them. Slide a short stem cover over the taped stems and glue the point of the stem cover to the underside of a leaf.

Align leaves with plant stem, wrap, and cover.

4. Continue combining leaves and flower clusters until all are connected to the central plant. Bend the leaves perpendicular to the stems.

5. Use the photograph of the finished plant (page 20) as a guide to shape and arrange the petals and leaves to simulate authentic blooms.

These beautiful red blossoms with their sumptuously bejeweled centers and upright stature can deliver a delightful promise of spring weeks before the first thaw. Arrange them in a pot with gravel or marbles and they can deceive even the most ardent horticulturist at twenty paces.

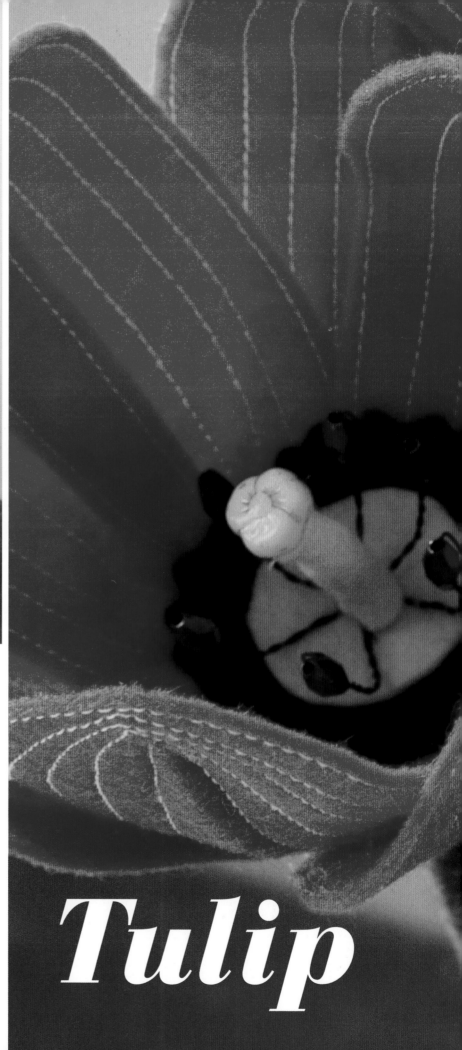

Tulip

materials

See pages 6–7 for basic supplies.

TO MAKE THE PLANT AS SHOWN, YOU WILL NEED:

RED FELT: 1 piece 18″ × 21″ for the flowers

DEEP VIOLET FELT: 1 piece 3″ × 7″ for the flower centers

BRIGHT YELLOW FELT: 1 piece 2″ × 4″ for the flower centers

PALE YELLOW FELT: 3 pieces, each 1½″ × 1″, for the flower stamens

LEAF GREEN FELT: 1 piece 18″ × 28″ for the leaves; 3 strips, each 1½″ × 17″, for the stem covers

¼″-DIAMETER STEM: 3 pieces, each 15″ long

18-GAUGE COVERED FLORIST WIRE: 16 pieces, each 4″ long, for the petals; 3 pieces, each 6″ long, for the flower centers; 9 pieces, each 9″ long, for the leaves

GREEN OVAL FACETED GLASS NOVELTY BEADS: 18

LARGE YELLOW GLASS FLOWER NOVELTY BEADS: 3

28-GAUGE PURPLE ANODIZED BEADING WIRE: 5 yards

FLORIST TAPE

fast2fuse DOUBLE-SIDED FUSIBLE STIFF INTERFACING OR OTHER STIFF INTERFACING: 1 piece 2″ × 6″

instructions

See pages 8–11 for basic techniques.

Make the Petals

1. Make templates for the Tulip petal, the small and large leaves, and the petal center using the patterns on the pullout.

2. Trace the petal template 16 times and the petal center template 16 times (6 times for each flower and 4 times for the bud) onto red felt. Transfer the top-stitching lines to the petals.

3. Cut out **only** the petal centers, and arrange them as shown on the petals. Stitch them in place close to the edges of the petal centers using contrasting yellow thread. Leave the lower edges open for inserting wire later. Stitch carefully around the outlines of the petals. Topstitch as indicated to create surface texture on the petals.

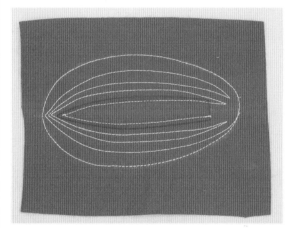

Stitch petal centers onto petals, then topstitch.

4. Cut out the stitched petals slightly beyond the outer stitching lines. Fold each petal in half lengthwise with right sides together (petal center on the outside). Stitch diagonally across the bottom of the petal just below the petal center on the dotted line drawn on the pattern. Trim off the lower edge of each petal slightly beyond the stitching.

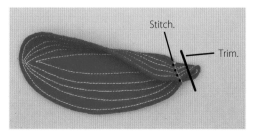

Fold petal lengthwise, and stitch diagonally.

5. Insert florist wire into the petal center. Cut the wire to fit the petal center pocket. Turn the lower edge of the petal inside out toward the wired petal center.

Insert wire, and cut to fit.

Turn lower edge.

Make the Leaves

1. Trace the large leaf template 6 times (twice for each flower) and the small leaf template 3 times (once for each flower) onto leaf green felt. Layer this marked felt with another piece of green felt.

2. Before cutting out each piece, stitch carefully around the outlines using coordinating thread. Topstitch as indicated to create surface texture. When topstitching the leaves, be sure to leave the center channels open at the base for interesting the wire. Cut out the leaves slightly beyond the outline stitching.

3. Insert florist wire into each leaf. Cut the wire close to the lower edge.

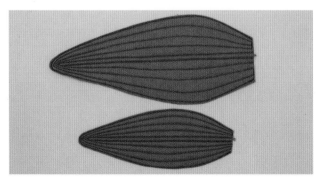

Stitch leaves, then cut out.

Make the Stems

1. Fold the stem covers in half lengthwise. Measure and stitch them to create a snug fit for the stems. Leave open about $1/2''$ at one end of each cover. Trim the seam allowances close to the stitching.

2. Slide the stem cover onto the stem, and glue it closed at the stitched end.

Make the Flower Centers

1. Insert a 6″ piece of beading wire through a large yellow flower bead. Fold the wire in half and twist it into a single strand. Repeat for the other yellow flower beads.

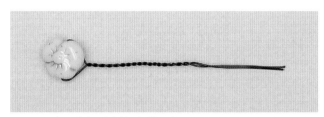

Insert wire through bead, fold in half, and twist.

2. Insert 6″ lengths of beading wire through each of the smaller faceted beads, fold each wire in half, and twist it together to form single strands.

3. Arrange a large yellow bead and one 6″ piece of florist wire on the pale yellow felt rectangle, with the bead extending just beyond the edge of the felt. Apply hot glue to secure the wires in place on the felt. Roll the felt around the wires, and glue it to form a tight cylinder that will be the stamen.

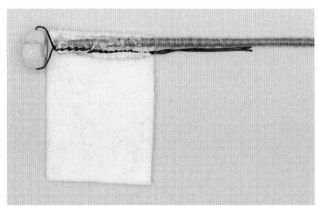

Glue wires to felt.

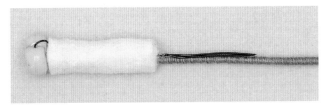

Roll felt into cylinder.

4. Arrange 6 smaller wired beads so they are spaced equally around the large yellow stamen. Twist the wire ends together around the florist wire, and wrap the wires with florist tape to secure them. Repeat Steps 3 and 4 to complete 3 beaded stamens.

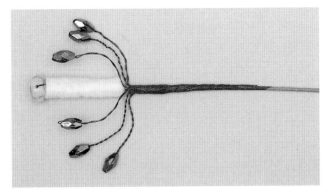

Arrange beads around center; secure wires with florist tape.

5. Cut 3 circles 2″ in diameter from the deep violet felt using a scallop-edge rotary cutter. Cut 3 circles 1″ in diameter from the bright yellow felt using scissors.

6. Center and glue a bright yellow felt circle onto each of the purple scalloped circles. Cut 3 circles 1¹/₂″ in diameter from the stiff interfacing and glue them onto the undersides of the purple scalloped circles. Cut a small slit through all the layers. Insert the florist wire with beaded stamens through the slit in the felt center so that the stamens sit firmly.

Insert florist wire with beaded stamens through slit in felt center.

Put the Plant Together

1. Slide the stem cover back a few inches from its open end, and align the flower center on top of the stem with the florist wire extending along the stem. Use florist tape to wrap the florist wire and stem tightly and smoothly together. Glue the underside of the flower center to the stem top to secure it. Slide the stem cover over the taped area, and glue it neatly to the underside of the flower center. Glue the seam completely closed.

2. Apply glue inside the lower curved edge of a petal and glue it to the underside of the flower center so that the petal is perpendicular to the flower center, as shown. Hold it in place until the glue is completely dry.

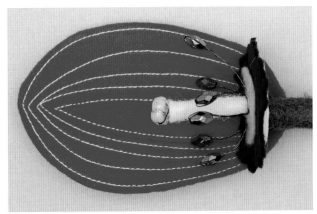

Glue petals to flower center.

3. Continue with 2 more petals, placing them so that the petal edges touch and completely cover the underside of the flower center. Hold them in place and allow the glue on each petal to dry completely before adding another petal.

4. Add 3 more petals in a second layer, so that they are centered equally over the edges of the previous layer, as shown.

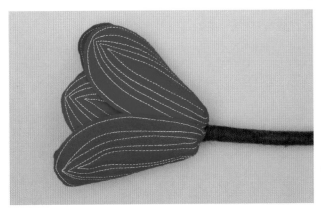

Glue second layer of petals overlapping edges of previous layer.

5. To make the bud, repeat the same process as described above, but use only 3 or 4 petals and shape the petals inward so that the flower is more tightly closed.

Make bud with 3 or 4 petals. Shape them inward.

6. To attach the leaves, apply glue in a triangle along the lower edge of a small leaf. Pinch the glued edges together tightly around the stem, about 5″ or 6″ below the flower. Attach the larger leaves in the same manner, in pairs about 4″ from the bottom of the stem.

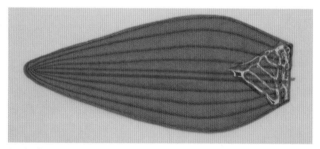

Apply glue in triangle.

Attach leaves in pairs on opposite sides of stem.

7. Use the photograph of the finished plant (page 24) as a guide to shape and arrange the petals and leaves to simulate authentic blooms.

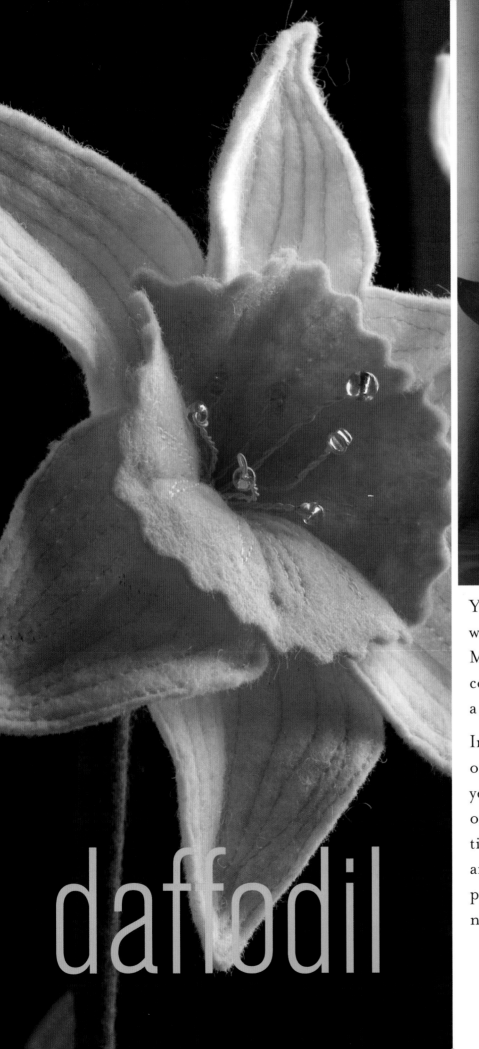

daffodil

You can celebrate spring anytime with these fresh, perky Daffodils. Make just a few to brighten a corner, or get crazy and make a whole basketful.

In nature, Daffodils come in lots of color variations, from the palest yellows and whites with vibrant orange centers to the more traditional bright yellow. These flowers are easy to make and are a great project to start with if you're new to fabric sculpting.

materials

See pages 6–7 for basic supplies.

FOR EACH FLOWER YOU WILL NEED:

WHITE FELT: 1 piece 6″ × 11″ for the petals

YELLOW FELT: 1 piece 4″ × 5″ for the flower center

DEEP GREEN FELT: 2 pieces, each 5″ × 14″, for the leaves; 1 piece 3″ × 4″ for the flower back; 1 strip 2″ × 17″ for the stem cover

¼″-DIAMETER STEM: 1 piece 15″ long

18-GAUGE COVERED FLORIST WIRE: 2 pieces, each 14″ long, for the leaves

26-GAUGE WHITE-COVERED FLORIST WIRE: 6 pieces, each 4″ long, for the petals

YELLOW-GREEN GLASS SEED BEADS: 6

YELLOW-GREEN GLASS E-BEAD: 1

WHITE OR GOLD-COLORED 28-GAUGE BEADING WIRE: 1 piece 24″ long

FLORIST TAPE

instructions

See pages 8–11 for basic techniques.

Make the Petals

1. Make templates for the Daffodil petals, flower center, flower back, and leaf using the patterns on the pullout.

2. Trace the flower template twice for each flower onto white felt. Transfer the topstitching lines.

3. **Before cutting out the petals,** stitch carefully around the outlines and top-stitch as indicated, using coordinating thread, to create surface texture on the flower petals. Cut out the petals slightly beyond the outline stitching.

*Topstitch petals **before** cutting.*

4. Fold each petal lengthwise, right sides together, along the center of the petal. Stitch along the fold to create a small curved dart from the tip of the petal to the center of the flower.

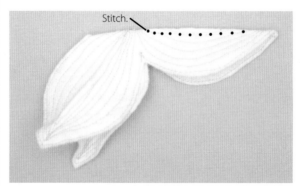

Sew small curved dart along center of petal.

5. Cut a small hole in the center of each petal set. Cut a small slit on the back in the center at the beginning of each dart. Insert a 4″ piece of florist wire into the channel created by each dart. Clip off the excess exposed wire.

Make the Flower Center and Back

1. Trace the flower back onto deep green felt. Trace the flower center onto yellow felt. Transfer the topstitching lines.

2. Topstitch using coordinating thread as indicated to create surface texture on the flower center. Cut around the curved outside edge using a scallop-edge rotary cutter. Cut straight across the straight edge. Mark the segments as indicated by the dotted lines on the template. Fold along a marked line, and topstitch from the center to the outer edge, close to the fold. Repeat for all the segments. Fold right sides together, aligning the 2 straight-cut edges. Stitch across edge, as before, to form final dart.

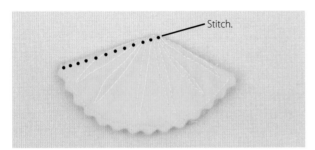

Flower center—stitch segments close to fold.

3. Use the same process as in Step 2 above to make the flower back. It will be shaped a little differently but is made basically the same way.

Flower back

Make the Leaves

1. Trace the leaf template twice for each flower onto deep green felt. Transfer the topstitching lines. Layer this marked felt with another piece of deep green felt.

2. **Before cutting out the leaves**, stitch around the outlines using coordinating thread, leaving them open along the bottom edges for inserting the wire. Stitch a channel through the center of each leaf for the wire. Topstitch as indicated.

3. Cut out the leaves slightly beyond the outline stitching and insert the covered florist wire through the channels in the leaves.

Cut out leaves and insert wire.

Make the Stem

1. Fold the stem cover in half lengthwise. Measure and stitch it to create a snug fit for the stem. Widen the stem cover at one end to approximately 1″ wide. Trim the seam allowance close to the stitching.

2. Cut across the wide end at an angle, as shown, after stitching.

Cut stem cover diagonally across widest point.

Make the Beaded Stamen

1. Fold the 24″ piece of beading wire in half to find the center. Thread the glass E-bead onto the center of the wire and twist the wire with needle-nose pliers to secure the bead.

2. Continue twisting to create a 2″ stem, then fold the wire about 2″ from the twist and thread on 1 of the smaller seed beads. Secure it with a twist. Create another twisted stem, and repeat until you have threaded all 6 small beads onto twisted wire stems.

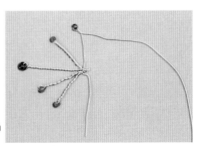

Thread beads onto wire, and twist.

3. Bring all the twisted ends together into a cluster, with the largest bead in the center. Twist them together at the opposite end from the beads.

Put the Flower Together

1. Cut a small hole in the center of the flower center. Thread the twisted stamen wires through the holes in the flower center and the 2 petal layers. Place a small drop of glue between the petal layers and the flower center to secure the stamens. Align the stamen wires with the stem at the back of the flower.

Glue petal layers and flower center.

2. Use florist tape to wrap the stem and stamen wires securely together.

Attach stamen wires to stem.

3. Slide the stem cover onto the stem, and glue it in place where the flower and the stem meet. Glue the other end neatly closed.

Glue stem cover in place.

4. To attach the flower back, cut a small hole at the center of the flower back and slide it onto the stem cover. Apply glue to the inside of the flower back and press it in place to attach it firmly to the back of the petals.

Attach flower back.

5. Glue the leaves in place along the stem so that the base of one leaf surrounds the stem and the second leaf surrounds the first leaf.

Glue leaves in place.

6. Use the photograph of the finished flowers (page 29) as a guide to shape and arrange the petals and leaves to simulate authentic blooms.

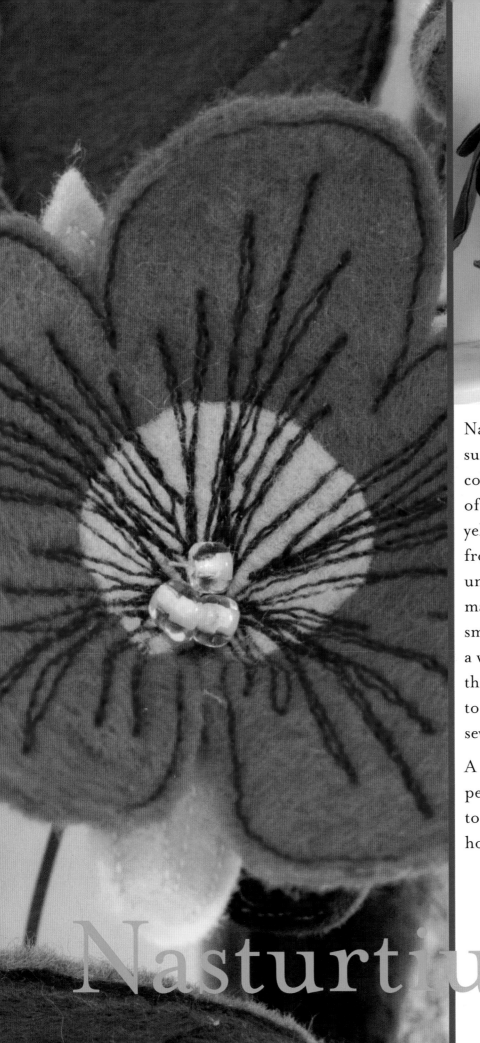

Nasturtiums are one of my favorite summer plants. Their brightly colored blooms come in a variety of colors, from red to orange to yellow. The blossoms peek out from under unusually shaped umbrella-like leaves, and they make a great hanging basket or small potted plant to brighten up a windowsill. Both the flowers and the leaves offer a great opportunity to practice your free-motion sewing skills.

A pot of these would make a perfectly memorable gift for you to share with a summertime hostess.

Nasturtium

materials

See pages 6–7 for basic supplies.

TO MAKE THE PLANT AS SHOWN, YOU WILL NEED:

RED-ORANGE FELT: 1 piece 8″ × 8″ for the flowers

MUSTARD YELLOW FELT: 1 piece 8″ × 10″ for the flower backs and the centers

LEAF GREEN FELT: 1 piece 13″ × 30″ for the leaves

GRAY-GREEN FELT: 1 piece 13″ × 30″ for the leaves

LARGE CLEAR YELLOW GLASS SEED BEADS: 15 for the flower centers

18-GAUGE COVERED FLORIST WIRE: 17 pieces, each 18″ long, for the leaves; 4 pieces, each 10″ long, for the flower back nectar tubes

FLORIST TAPE

instructions

See pages 8–11 for basic techniques.

Make the Flowers

1. Make templates for the Nasturtium flower; the small, medium, and large leaves; the flower back; and the flower center using the patterns on the pullout.

2. Trace the flower template 3 times (once for each flower) onto red-orange felt. Transfer the topstitching lines.

3. Trace the flower back and flower center 3 times each (once for each flower) onto a single layer of mustard felt. Transfer the topstitching lines. Cut out the flower centers **only**.

4. **Before cutting out the flower petals**, arrange the flower centers onto the petals and topstitch as indicated, with contrasting thread, to create surface texture on the flower petals. Stitch carefully around the outlines.

*Topstitch petals **before** cutting.*

5. Cut out the flowers slightly beyond the outline stitching.

6. Hand stitch 3 glass seed beads onto the center of each flower.

Hand stitch beads onto flower center.

7. **Before cutting out the flower backs**, stitch carefully around the outline and topstitch as indicated with coordinating thread. Cut out the flower backs slightly beyond the outline stitching.

8. Fold each flower back in half. Use coordinating thread and stitch together the edges of one folded petal along the dotted line drawn on the pattern from the flower back center to the point of the petal to form the nectar tube.

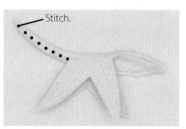

Stitch together edges of folded petal.

9. Bend a crook at one end of a 10″ length of florist wire. Insert the crook into the nectar tube, and glue the wire to secure it.

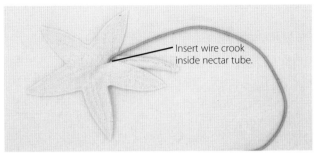

Insert wire into nectar tube, and glue.

10. Bring together the petals to form a round 5-petal flower, and glue the petals together onto the flower back so the points of the flower back are visible between the petals, as shown.

Glue petals to flower back.

11. To make the bud, trace, stitch, and cut out a piece for a Nasturtium flower. Don't bother about adding the center—it won't show. Sew and cut a Nasturtium flower back. Insert florist wire into the nectar tube in a similar manner as for the flowers. Roll the petals into a tight bud and glue the flower back around the petals to secure them.

Nasturtium bud

Make the Leaves

1. Trace the large leaf template 5 times, the medium leaf template 7 times, and the small leaf template 5 times onto leaf green felt. Transfer the topstitching lines. Layer this marked felt with a piece of gray-green felt.

2. **Before cutting out the leaves,** outline stitch and top-stitch with coordinating thread to create the veins on the leaves, being careful to leave the center channels open for inserting the florist wire.

Topstitch to create veins and wire channel.

3. Cut out the leaves slightly beyond the stitching. Turn over each leaf onto the gray-green side and cut a small hole in the center of the leaf at the beginning of the channel. Insert an 18″ piece of covered florist wire through the channel in the leaf and secure it with a small drop of glue. Bend the wire so that it extends directly down, perpendicular to the leaf surface, from the center of the leaf.

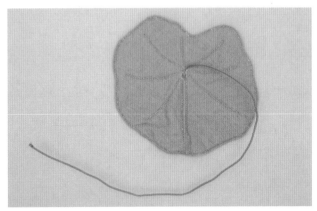

Insert wire and glue in place.

Put the Plant Together

1. Gather together the flowers and leaves in a cluster so that the largest leaves are near the bottom, and the flowers hover slightly above the leaves. Wrap the cluster of wire ends with florist tape to form a small plant.

2. Use the photograph of the finished flowers (page 33) as a guide to shape and arrange the petals and leaves to simulate authentic blooms.

These simple and graceful
blooms will add elegance
to any decor, from classical to
contemporary. A single Calla
Lily in a beautiful slender bud
vase makes a stunning visual
accent, but these flowers are
so easy to make that you might
get carried away and create a
sumptuous bouquet for the
ultimate in botanical opulence.

Calla Lily

materials

See pages 6–7 for basic supplies.

FOR EACH FLOWER YOU WILL NEED:

WHITE OR IVORY FELT: 2 pieces, each 8″ × 8″, for the flower

YELLOW FELT: 2 pieces, each ³/₄″ × 3¹/₂″, for the stamen

BASIL GREEN FELT: 1 strip 1¹/₂″ × 24″ for the flower stem cover

FOREST GREEN FELT: 2 pieces, each 6″ × 11″, for the leaves; 1 strip 1¹/₂″ × 24″ for the leaf stem cover

CREAMY YELLOW FAUX SUEDE FRINGE: 1 strip 1″ × 2″ for the flower (I use Wright's. See Resources, page 79, or page 11 to make your own.)

¹/₄″-DIAMETER STEM: 2 pieces, each 24″ long

18-GAUGE COVERED FLORIST WIRE: 1 piece 12″ long for the flower; 1 piece 14″ long for the leaf

instructions

See pages 8–11 for basic techniques.

Make the Petal, Leaf, and Stamen

1. Make templates for the Calla Lily petal, stamen, and leaf using the patterns on the pullout.

2. Trace the flower template once for each flower onto white felt. Transfer the topstitching lines. Layer this marked felt with another piece of white felt.

3. Trace the stamen template once for each flower onto yellow felt. Layer this marked felt with another piece of yellow felt.

4. Trace the leaf template once for each leaf onto forest green felt. Transfer the topstitching lines. Layer this marked felt with another piece of forest green felt.

5. **Before cutting out each piece**, stitch carefully around the outlines, using coordinating thread for the petals and stamen and contrasting thread for the leaf. Topstitch as indicated to create surface texture on the flower petals and veins on the leaves. When topstitching the leaves, be sure to leave the center channels open at the bases of the leaves for inserting the wire. Leave the stamens open across the bottom also.

6. Cut out each piece slightly beyond the outline stitching.

Stitch leaves and petals, then cut out.

7. Insert the covered florist wire through the channel in the leaf and glue the wire to secure it.

Insert wire.

8. Cut a $1/2'' \times 2''$ rectangle from the white felt scraps and glue it around the end of a wire piece to create a padded stamen base. Slide the stamen onto the padded wire and glue it in place. Wrap and glue the fringe around the cut end of the stamen.

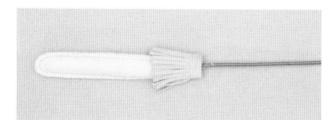

Wrap fringe.

9. Attach the stamen to the stem by wrapping the stamen wire around the top of the stem and gluing it in place.

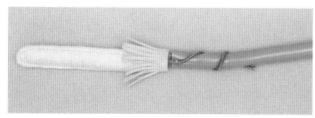

Attach stamen to stem.

10. Place a dab of glue in the center of the curved edge of the Calla Lily petal. Attach it to the stamen. Wrap the petal around the stamen, overlapping the curved edges to create a cone shape. Glue it closed. Let the glue dry completely.

 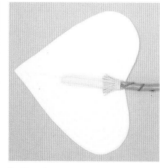

Apply glue.   *Position stamen.*

Wrap petal around stamen and glue closed.

Make the Stems

1. Fold each stem cover in half lengthwise. Measure and stitch to create a snug fit for the stems. Trim the seam allowance close to the stitching.

2. Slide the basil green stem cover onto the flower stem and glue it in place at the base of the flower, covering the point at which the flower meets the stem.

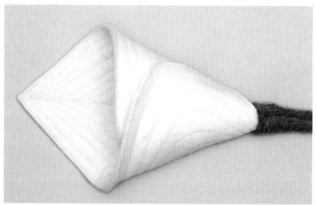

Glue stem cover to base of flower.

3. For the leaf, insert the stem and the wire extending from the leaf into the forest green stem cover. Glue carefully at the point where the leaf and the stem meet.

Glue stem cover inside leaf.

4. To finish the stem ends, trim away the excess fabric, and glue the edges closed.

5. Use the photograph of the finished flowers (page 36) as a guide to shape and arrange the petals and leaves to simulate authentic blooms. Be sure to fold back the edges of the flower to create a dimensional effect.

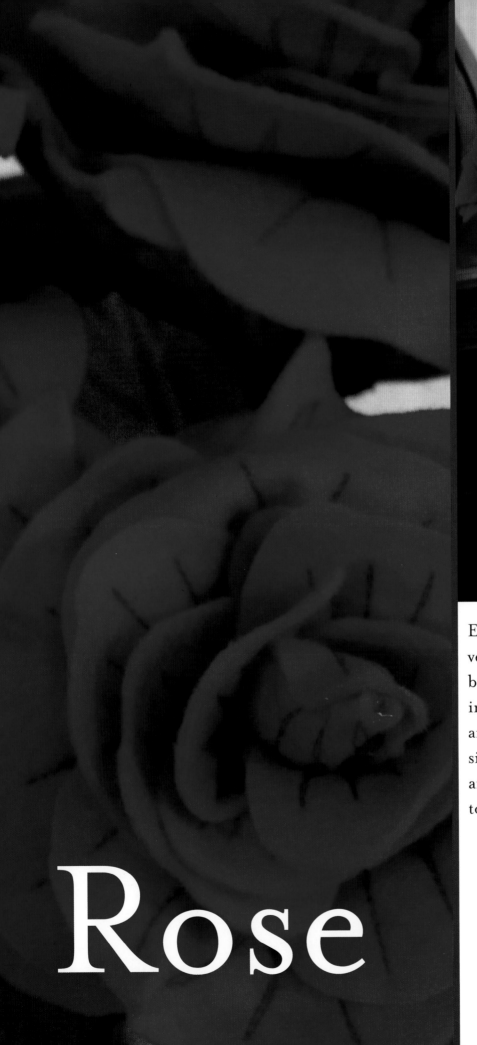

Rose

Everyone's favorite, these velvety Roses make a beautiful bouquet to be enjoyed year-round in any setting. A single bloom in an elegant silver bud vase looks simply elegant, or you can create an opulent display that's glorious to behold.

materials

See pages 6–7 for basic supplies.

FOR EACH FLOWER YOU WILL NEED:

RED FELT: 1 piece 10″ × 19″ for the petals

LEAF GREEN FELT: 1 piece 6″ × 8″ for the leaves;
1 piece 5″ × 5″ for the flower back

FOREST GREEN FELT: 1 piece 6″ × 8″ for the
leaves; 1 strip 1$\frac{1}{2}$″ × 17″ for the stem cover

$\frac{1}{4}$″-DIAMETER STEM: 1 piece 15″ long

18-GAUGE COVERED FLORIST WIRE: 2 pieces, each
7″ long, for the leaves

FIBERFILL: a small amount for the bud

instructions

See pages 8–11 for basic techniques.

Make the Petals and Leaves

1. Make templates for the Rose flower center, small and large petals, flower back, and leaf using the patterns on the pullout.

2. Trace the flower templates onto red felt. For each flower trace a flower center, 2 small petals, and 3 large petals. Transfer the topstitching lines.

3. Trace the flower back template onto leaf green felt. Transfer the topstitching lines.

4. Trace the leaf template twice for each flower onto leaf green felt. Transfer the topstitching lines. Layer this marked felt with a piece of forest green felt.

5. Before cutting out each piece, topstitch as indicated with coordinating thread for the petals and center and contrasting thread for the leaves and flower back. This creates surface texture on the flower petals and flower back, and veins on the leaves. When topstitching the leaves, be sure to leave the center channels open at the bases of the leaves for inserting the wire.

6. Cut out each piece just inside the traced outlines. Use pinking shears or a scallop-edge rotary blade to create sawtooth edges on the leaves.

Stitch petals, flower back, and leaves, then cut out.

7. Insert wire through the channels in the leaves.

Insert wire.

Make the Stem

1. Fold the stem cover in half lengthwise. Measure and stitch it to create a snug fit for the stem. Trim the seam allowance close to the stitching.

2. Cut a 4″ length of the stem cover diagonally. Slide this short piece of the stem cover onto the upper stem and glue it in place.

Put the Flower Together

1. Wrap and glue the fiberfill into a small cone shape at the covered end of the stem. Apply glue to one side of the flower center, and pinch the tip ends together, encasing the batting. Apply glue to the other half of the flower center, and fold it around the first half, leaving the upper tip of the petal slightly open as in a live rosebud.

Glue batting to stem.

Glue one side of flower center around batting.

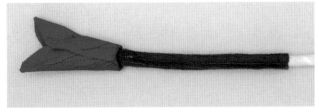

Finish with upper tip slightly open.

2. Begin wrapping and gluing smaller petals in a circular pattern onto the flower center, pinching the bases of the petals to fit them around the base of the center. Continue with larger petals until all the petals are glued onto the center.

Glue petals in place.

3. To add dimension to the Rose petals, place a small amount of glue onto a straight pin and apply it randomly to the underside of the large petals while pinching together the edges from the upper side.

Glue petals and pinch together to add dimension.

4. Glue the flower back at the point where the flower meets the stem.

5. Arrange the leaves onto the stem at the point where the short stem cover ends, and glue them in place. Slide the remaining stem cover onto the stem and carefully glue it in place, covering the point where the leaves are attached. The diagonal point of the stem cover extends above the leaves toward the rose. Glue the other end of the stem cover neatly closed.

Attach leaves and stem cover.

Diagonal point of stem cover

6. Use the photograph of the finished flowers (page 39) as a guide to shape and arrange the petals and leaves to simulate authentic blooms.

These spectacular giant Sunflowers
are bound to become the focal
point of any decor, whether casual
or dramatic. Shown here in rich
wine red, they can also be made
in the more traditional gold and
orange tones for a warm sunny
display.

Sunflower

materials

See pages 6–7 for basic supplies.

FOR EACH FLOWER YOU WILL NEED:

WINE FELT: 3 pieces, each 12″ × 12″, for the flower petals

LEAF GREEN FELT: 3 pieces 12″ × 12″ for the flower petals; 2 pieces 8″ × 12″ for the leaves and back; 1 strip 4″ × 26″ for the stem cover

FOREST GREEN FELT: 2 pieces 8″ × 12″ for the leaves and back; 1 piece, 5″ × 5″ for the flower center

1″-DIAMETER STEM: 1 piece 24″ long

18-GAUGE COVERED FLORIST WIRE: 32 pieces, each 3″ long, for the petals; 2 pieces, each 6″ long, for the leaves

DOUBLE-SIDED ADHESIVE: 4″ × 4″ (This needs to be very strong. I recommend SuperTape by Therm O Web.)

fast2fuse DOUBLE-SIDED FUSIBLE STIFF INTERFACING: 1 piece 4″ × 6″ for the stem joint

SEED BEADS: 2 yards strung onto monofilament or beading thread for the flower center

BUGLE OR SEED BEADS: 1/2 oz in coordinating colors for the flower center

instructions

See pages 8–11 for basic techniques.

Make the Petals, Leaves, and Flower Back

1. Make templates for the Sunflower center and petals, flower back, stem joint, and leaf using the patterns on the pullout.

2. Trace the flower template once for each flower onto a piece of wine felt. Transfer the topstitching lines. Trace the flower template again once for each flower onto another piece of wine felt. Transfer the topstitching lines. Layer this second piece of marked felt with another piece of wine felt. You will have a flower petal tracing on a single layer of wine felt and a flower petal tracing on a double layer of wine felt.

Repeat the same process tracing the flower template onto leaf green felt. You will have flower petal tracings on a single layer and on a double layer of leaf green felt.

3. Trace the Sunflower back once for each flower onto leaf green felt. Transfer the topstitching lines. Layer this marked felt with another piece of leaf green felt.

4. Trace the leaf template twice for each flower onto leaf green felt. Transfer the topstitching lines. Layer this marked felt with a piece of forest green felt.

5. **Before cutting out the petals,** stitch carefully around the outlines of the flower, using coordinating thread, and topstitch as indicated to create surface texture on the flower petals. When topstitching, be sure to leave the center channels open at the bases of the double-layered petals for inserting wire.

Stitch petals and leaves, then cut out.

6. Carefully cut out the flowers slightly beyond the outline stitching. Use a rotary cutter to ensure clean cutting lines between petals.

7. For the single-layered petals, fold each petal in half and stitch from the tip to the center, creating a small dart that will shape the petal.

Stitch.

Dart

Stitch dart in each petal.

8. For the double-layered petals, cut away one layer of the flower center slightly inside the stitching, and insert a piece of florist wire into the channel of each petal. Clip the wire close to the stitching.

Cut away one layer and insert florist wire into center channel of each petal.

9. **Before cutting out the leaves**, topstitch as indicated with coordinating thread, and stitch around the outlines of the leaves, being careful to leave open the channel at the bottom center of each leaf for inserting wire.

10. Carefully cut out the leaves slightly beyond the outline stitching using a scallop-edge rotary cutter. Insert covered florist wire through the channel in the leaf.

Insert wire.

11. Before cutting out the flower back, topstitch as indicated to create texture all over the flower back, and stitch around the outline. Cut out the flower back slightly beyond the outline stitching.

Make the Stem

1. Fold the stem cover in half lengthwise. Measure and stitch it to create a snug fit for the stem. Trim the seam allowance close to the stitching.

2. Slide the stem cover onto the stem, and glue it closed at one end.

Make the Flower Center

1. Apply the double-sided adhesive to the remaining piece of dark green felt and cut out a 3³/₄″-diameter circle for the flower center.

2. Peel away the protective covering from the top of the double-sided adhesive covering the felt flower center.

3. Beginning at the center of the circle and working outward, coil the seed beads tightly, pressing the beads into the adhesive until all the beads are securely attached. Sprinkle bugle or seed beads solidly, but randomly, around the remaining outer edges of the flower center and press firmly to adhere them.

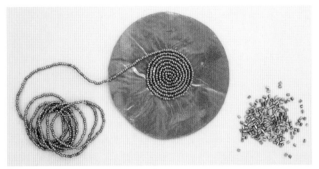

Coil and adhere bugle beads onto double-sided adhesive.

Put the Flower Together

1. Arrange and glue the flower layers together so that the points of one layer fall between the petals of the previous layer. Apply the glue to the flower centers only, leaving the petals free. Start with the single green petals on the bottom, followed by the wired green petals. Add the wired wine petals, ending with the single wine petals on top, with the darts facing down.

Stack, arrange, and glue flower petals.

2. Glue the beaded flower center to the center of the top layer.

Glue beaded center to top layer.

3. Trace the stem joint onto fast2fuse. Cut out the stem joint, cutting slits as indicated.

4. Turn the Sunflower facedown and center the stem on the back side of the flower. Apply glue generously to attach the stem to the flower. Hold it in place steadily until the glue is completely set. Glue the stem joint around the point where the stem meets the flower. Hold the stem in place until the glue is dry.

Glue stem in place and secure with stem joint.

5. Apply glue to one side of the flower back and arrange it around the stem and onto the back side of the flower, covering the stem joint completely.

Wrap and glue flower back around stem.

6. Apply glue to the lower edge of one leaf and glue it onto the stem about 6″ below the flower. Glue the other leaf on the opposite side of the stem at the same distance below the flower.

Apply glue.

Glue leaves in place.

7. Use the photograph of the finished flowers (page 43) as a guide to shape and arrange the petals and leaves to simulate authentic blooms.

gladiolus

A favorite in summertime gardens, Gladioli come in every imaginable color and provide dramatic feathery blooms, unfurling up a tall stem, topped off by tightly wound buds that promise to open soon. Accompanied by tall green strap leaves, these flamboyant florals will add a festive touch to your decor.

materials

See pages 6–7 for basic supplies.

FOR EACH STALK YOU WILL NEED:

RED FELT: 1 piece 14″ × 18″ for the flowers

LEAF GREEN FELT: 2 pieces, each 7″ × 20″, for the large leaves; 1 piece 12″ × 15″ for the small leaves; 1 strip 1¹⁄₂″ × 26″ for the stem cover

¹⁄₄″-DIAMETER STEM: 1 piece 24″ long

18-GAUGE COVERED FLORIST WIRE: 5 pieces, each 6″ long, for the flowers and the buds; 2 pieces, each 18″ long, for the large leaves

28-GAUGE BEADING WIRE IN SEVERAL COLORS: 6 pieces, each 4″ long, for the stamens

SMALL GREEN OR YELLOW OVAL GLASS NOVELTY BEADS: 6 for the stamens

instructions

See pages 8–11 for basic techniques.

Make the Flowers, Buds, and Leaves

1. Make templates for the Gladiolus flower and small and large leaves using the patterns on the pullout.

2. Trace the flower template 4 times for each stalk onto red felt. Transfer the topstitching lines.

3. **Before cutting out the flowers,** topstitch as indicated with contrasting thread to create surface texture on the flower petals. Cut out carefully just inside the traced outlines.

Stitch petals, then cut out.

4. Trace the large leaf template twice for each stalk onto leaf green felt. Transfer the topstitching lines. Layer this marked felt with another piece of leaf green felt.

5. Trace the small leaf template 10 times for each stalk onto leaf green felt. Transfer the topstitching lines.

6. **Before cutting out the leaves,** stitch carefully around the outlines, using coordinating thread, and topstitch as indicated to create surface texture and veins on the leaves. Be sure to leave the center channels open at the bases of the large leaves for inserting wire. Cut out the leaves carefully, slightly beyond the stitching.

Stitch leaves, then cut out.

7. Insert the covered florist wire through the channels in the large leaves.

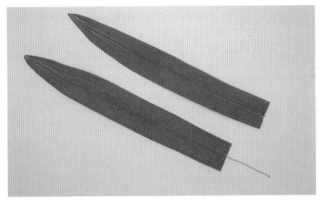

Insert wire.

8. To make the stamen, thread the beading wire through the glass beads. Bend the wire in half, and twist the bead while holding the wire ends together with needle-nose pliers to entwine the wires. Twist together 6 stamens for the large flower and 2 stamens for the smaller flower. Randomly use different colors of beading wire for added texture.

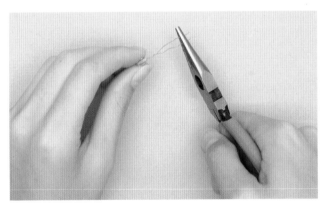

Twist bead to entwine wires.

9. Gather together the stamen wires and twist them around one end of a 6˝ piece of florist wire. Cut a ³/₄˝ × ³/₄˝ square of green felt from scraps, and glue it snugly around the point at which the stamen and florist wire meet.

Wrap stamen around florist wire.

Glue felt around stamen.

10. To assemble the flowers, place the stamen at the center lower edge of the right petal and glue the petal around the green felt. Repeat with the left petal, leaving the center petal free. Wrap and glue the center petal around the base of the previously glued petals. For the larger flower, add a second layer of petals, centering the petals between those in the previous layer. To finish the flower, wrap and glue a small green leaf around the base of the flower, covering the lower edge of the petals but leaving the florist wire exposed.

Glue right petal around green felt.

Repeat with left petal.

Glue center petal and add leaf around base.

11. To make the buds, cut apart one flower into 3 separate petals. Place a piece of florist wire at the lower edge of each petal and glue it, wrapping the petal around the wires to create a tight cone-shaped bud. Glue and wrap one of the small leaves around each bud to cover the point at which the wire extends from the bud.

Wrap leaf around bud.

Make the Stem

1. Fold the stem cover in half lengthwise. Measure and stitch it to create a snug fit for the stem. Trim the seam allowance close to the stitching.

2. Slide the stem cover onto the stem, and glue it closed at the ends.

Put the Stalk Together

1. To begin assembling the stalk, wrap the florist wire from one bud around the top of the stem, and glue it in place. Wrap and glue a small leaf so that it covers the base of the bud.

Attach bud to top of stem and wrap leaf around base.

2. Continuing down the stem, glue another bud on the opposite side of the main stem and cover it with a leaf, this time covering both the base of the previous leaf and the stem.

3. Attach the third bud and leaf, then the smaller flower, covering the base and stem with an additional small leaf, and finally the larger flower and the remaining small leaf.

Attach flowers to stem.

4. To attach the large strap leaves, apply a bead of glue along one leaf, starting at the center and extending out at the lower edge. Fold the leaf around the stem and glue the edges together. Repeat with the other leaf, and glue it opposite the previous leaf. Let the glue dry completely.

Apply glue.

Attach large leaves to stem.

5. Use the photograph of the finished flowers as a guide to shape and arrange the petals and leaves to simulate authentic blooms.

This stately and mysterious flower and bud evoke memories of the fragrant gardens of my Southern childhood. Thick, fleshy petals surround a creamy multilayered center. The flower and bud are framed by deep forest green and rust leaves.

Place the branch on your mantel for an elegant holiday display, or arrange it in a tall vase for a sumptuous centerpiece that's sure to spark conversation at your next dinner party.

Magnolia

materials

See pages 6–7 for basic supplies.

TO MAKE THE FLOWER AND BUD AS SHOWN, YOU
WILL NEED:

WHITE OR IVORY FELT: 2 pieces, each 18″ × 40″,
for the petals

LEMON FELT: 1 piece 3″ × 8″ for the flower
center

PEACH FELT: 1 piece 3″ × 8″ for the flower
center

FOREST GREEN FELT: 1 piece 10″ × 25″ for the
leaves

RUST FELT: 1 piece 10″ × 25″ for the leaves

DARK BROWN FELT: 2 strips, each 2″ × 26″, for
the flower stem covers

CREAMY YELLOW FAUX SUEDE FRINGE:
2 pieces, each 1¹/₂″, for the flower centers
(I use Wright's. See Resources, page 79, or
page 11 to make your own.)

¹/₄″-DIAMETER STEM: 2 pieces, each 24″ long

18-GAUGE COVERED FLORIST WIRE:
5 pieces, each 18″ long, for the leaves

FLORIST TAPE

instructions

See pages 8–11 for basic techniques.

Make the Petals

1. Make templates for the Magnolia small and large petal, flower center, and small and large leaves using the patterns on the pullout.

2. Trace the large and small petal template 12 times each onto white felt. Transfer the topstitching lines. Layer this marked felt with another piece of white felt.

3. **Before cutting out the flower petals,** stitch carefully around the out-lines, using coordinating thread, and topstitch as indicated to create sur-face texture on the flower petals. Be careful to leave a channel for inserting florist wire as indicated on one half of each petal.

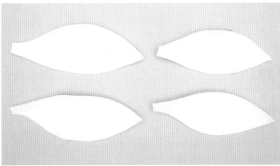
Stitch petals, then cut out.

Cut out the flower petals slightly beyond the outline stitching.

4. Match the centers of pairs of top-stitched petals, and stitch from top to bottom with a zigzag stitch set at about 2.5 length and 3.0 width to join the petal halves together. (See Flat-Joining Seams, page 10.) Because you are joining curved edges, the finished petals will have a cuplike shape. Insert florist wire into the channels and trim at top lower edge of the petals.

Match pairs and zigzag stitch to join petal halves.

Make the Flower Center

1. Align the flower center template along one edge of the lemon felt and trace the jagged template edge. Repeat along the other edge (see page 9 for inter-locking pattern layouts). Mark the topstitching lines. Layer this marked felt with a piece of peach felt.

2. **Before cutting,** stitch along all traced lines with coordinating thread. Cut out slightly beyond the stitching along the points.

3. Apply glue to one end of the stem and fold 2 flower center points over the stem end, matching the points. Continue wrapping and gluing so that the points overlap the previous layer, as shown. Repeat to make a second flower center stem for the bud.

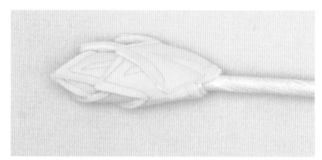

Points overlap previous layers.

4. Finish the flower centers by wrapping and gluing the fringe tightly around the bottom edge of each flower center, covering the point at which it meets the stem wire.

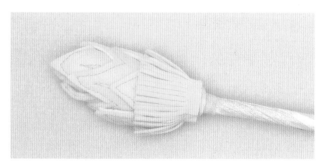

Wrap and glue fringe around flower center.

Make the Leaves

1. Trace the small leaf template 2 times and the large leaf template 3 times onto forest green felt. Layer this marked felt with a piece of rust felt.

2. Before cutting out the leaves, stitch carefully around the outlines using contrasting thread for each pair of fabrics (rust thread on green and green thread on rust). Don't leave any openings; the wire channel is created below in Step 4.

3. Transfer the interior topstitching lines, and topstitch the interior lines using **matching** thread (rust on rust, green on green) to create the veins on the leaves. (To avoid rethreading your machine or rewinding your bobbin, simply flip the piece over to mark and stitch.) Cut out the leaves slightly beyond the outline stitching.

Topstitch to create veins on leaves, then cut out.

4. Fold each leaf in half lengthwise, with the green on the inside. Stitch a channel close to the fold with a seam allowance that is wide enough for a piece of florist wire to slide into. Taper the channel to a point at the top of the leaf. Insert the covered florist wire through the channel in the leaf, leaving the wire extending 3″ from the end of the leaf.

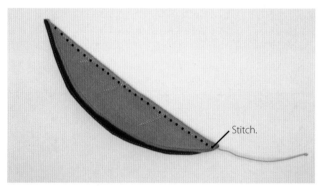

Insert wire through channel.

Make the Stems

1. Fold each stem cover in half lengthwise. Measure and stitch it to create a snug fit for the stem. Taper the stem cover outward at one end to the widest point.

2. Trim the seam allowance close to the stitching.

Put the Plant Together

1. Apply glue to the end of one small petal and glue it in place around the flower center, just below the fringe.

Glue petal to flower center.

2. Continue gluing 2 more small petals, overlapping the previous petal by one half so that the 3 petals completely encase the flower center. Repeat with 6 large petals to complete the large flower.

Glue petals in place.

3. To make the bud, use 3 small petals and wrap the first one tightly around the flower center. Fold the second petal completely around the first, and then add the third petal so that the bud appears to be just beginning to open.

4. To attach the leaves, arrange 2 large leaves and 1 small leaf around the flower. Wrap the florist wire extensions around the bare stem. Then wrap the wires and stem with florist tape to secure them. Pull up the stem cover over the wrapped area and glue it carefully to join the stem cover edges to the undersides of the leaves, as shown. Glue the other end neatly closed.

Wrap wires around stem.   *Secure with florist tape.*

Glue stem cover to underside of leaves.

5. Repeat the same process for the bud, using 1 small and 1 large leaf.

Completed bud

6. Make extra leaves as desired.

7. Use the photograph of the finished flowers (page 52) as a guide to shape and arrange the petals and leaves to simulate authentic blooms.

Although Irises grow in all sorts
of unusual colors, with seem-
ingly endless variations such as
fuzzy beards and frilly ruffles,
this classic Dutch Iris is my all-
time favorite. It is said to be the
origin of the fleur-de-lis, often
used in heraldry.

The blossom is so stately that
one simple bloom with leaves
and a bud creates a lovely accent
for a small table. However,
if you prefer, you can make
several of these lovely blooms to
add striking touches of purple
to a mixed spring bouquet of
tulips and daffodils.

iris

materials

See pages 6–7 for basic supplies.

TO MAKE ONE FLOWER WITH A BUD AND LEAVES, YOU WILL NEED:

LIGHT VIOLET FELT: 1 piece 4″ × 5″ for the petal center covers

VIOLET FELT: 2 pieces, each 5″ × 12″, for the petals

LEAF GREEN FELT: 2 pieces, each 8″ × 18″, for the leaves; 1 piece 5″ × 5″ for the flower and the bud backs; 1 strip 2″ × 17″ for the stem cover

¼″-DIAMETER STEM: 1 piece 15″ long

26-GAUGE COVERED FLORIST WIRE: 2 pieces, each 18″ long, for the large leaves; 9 pieces, each 8″ long, for the petals and small leaves

FLORIST TAPE

instructions

See pages 8–11 for basic techniques.

Make the Petals and Leaves

1. Make templates for the Iris small and large petals, the petal center cover, the flower back, the bud back, and the small and large leaves using the patterns on the pullout.

2. Trace the large petal template 3 times (for the flower) and the small petal template 4 times (3 for the flower and 1 for the bud) onto violet felt. Transfer the topstitching lines. Layer this marked felt with another piece of violet felt.

3. Trace the petal center cover 3 times onto light violet felt. Transfer the topstitching lines.

4. Trace the large and small leaf templates 2 times each onto leaf green felt. Transfer the topstitching lines. Layer this marked felt with another piece of leaf green felt.

5. Trace the flower back and the bud back once each onto leaf green felt.

6. **Before cutting out each piece,** stitch carefully around the outlines, using coordinating thread for the petals, leaves, and flower backs. Use contrasting thread for the petal centers. Topstitch as indicated to create surface texture on the flower petals and centers, and the veins on the leaves. When topstitching the petals and leaves, be sure to leave the center channels open at the lower edges for inserting wire. Cut out the pieces slightly beyond the outline stitching.

Stitch petals and leaves, then cut out.

7. Insert an 8″ length of covered florist wire into the channel of each petal. The wires will extend from the bases of the petals.

8. Insert the florist wire into the center channels in the leaves and cut to fit.

Insert wires into petals.

Make the Stem

1. Fold the stem cover in half lengthwise. Measure and stitch it to create a snug fit for the stem. Trim the seam allowance close to the stitching.

2. Slide the stem cover onto the stem, and glue it closed at one end, leaving the other end open for attaching the flower later.

Put the Plant Together

1. Carefully arrange and glue the center petal covers onto the large petals, leaving the tops of the petal covers free. Allow the glue to dry completely.

Glue center petal covers.

2. Gather the 3 large petals together and arrange them so that they are evenly spaced and the bases of the petals meet in the center. Add the smaller petals, spacing them between the large petals to form the flower. Twist together the florist wires.

Gather petals together and twist wires to form flower.

3. Slide the stem cover back several inches, and align the twisted petal wires and the stem. Wrap the wires and stem with florist tape. Slide the stem cover back in place over the taped area, and glue the stem cover to the flower at the point where they meet.

4. Apply glue to the flower back, and glue it to the back of the flower, covering the stem end and aligning each point on the flower back with one of the petals.

Align points on flower back with petals.

5. To make the bud, fold the remaining small petal in half. Apply a drop of glue in the center, place a piece of florist wire on the glue, and roll the petal together tightly to form a small bud. Glue the bud back around the point at which the florist wire extends from the bud. Trim the florist wire to 2″.

Make bud by rolling folded petal.

Add bud back.

6. Apply a small line of glue along the lower center of a small leaf, and glue the bud stem in place. Fold the leaf around the flower stem about 4″ below the flower and pinch together the edges of the leaf so that it extends at a slight angle out from the stem. Wrap and glue the remaining small leaf over the point at which the first one is attached to the stem.

Glue bud to small leaf.

Attach bud to stem.

Add another small leaf.

7. Apply glue along the bottom inch of one of the long strap leaves and glue it in place by wrapping it around the bottom of the stem. Wrap and glue the other long leaf around the base so that the stem appears to grow out from between the leaves.

Wrap and glue long leaves around stem.

8. Use the photograph of the finished flowers (page 56) as a guide to shape and arrange the petals and leaves to simulate authentic blooms.

The tall spiky blooms of
the Ginger plant are great for
punctuating a tropical bouquet.
You can make them up in
vibrant reds and oranges, or,
if you prefer, try pairing contrasting shades of luscious pink
and deep wine. Either way, these
impressive blossoms are much
easier to make than they appear.

Ginger

materials

See pages 6–7 for basic supplies.

FOR EACH FLOWER YOU WILL NEED:

ORANGE FELT: 1 piece 5″ × 9″ for the small petals

RED FELT: 1 piece 5″ × 9″ for the small petals

CRANBERRY FELT: 1 piece 6″ × 13″ for the large petals

WINE FELT: 1 piece 6″ × 13″ for the large petals; 1 strip 1 1/2″ × 32″ for the stem cover

BASIL GREEN FELT: 1 piece 6″ × 14″ for the leaf

FOREST GREEN FELT: 1 piece 6″ × 14″ for the leaf

1/4″-DIAMETER STEM: 1 piece 30″ long

18-GAUGE COVERED FLORIST WIRE: 1 piece 13″ long for the leaf

instructions

See pages 8–11 for basic techniques.

Make the Petals and Leaf

1. Make templates for the Ginger small and large petals and leaf using the patterns on the pullout.

2. Trace the small flower template once for each flower onto orange felt. Transfer the topstitching lines. Layer this marked felt with a piece of red felt.

3. Trace the large flower template once for each flower onto cranberry felt. Transfer the topstitching lines. Layer this marked felt with a piece of wine felt.

4. Trace the leaf template once onto basil green felt. Transfer the topstitching lines. Layer this marked felt with a piece of forest green felt.

5. **Before cutting out each piece,** stitch carefully around the outlines using coordinating thread for the leaves and contrasting thread for the petals. Topstitch as indicated to create surface texture on the flower petals and veins on the leaves. When topstitching the leaves, be sure to leave the center channels open at the bases of the leaves for inserting the wire.

6. Cut out the leaves and petals slightly beyond the outline stitching.

7. Insert the covered florist wire through the channel in each leaf.

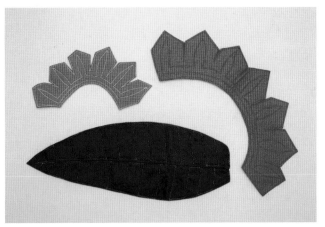

Stitch leaves and petals, then cut out and insert wire.

Make the Stem

1. Fold the stem cover in half lengthwise. Measure and stitch it to create a snug fit for the stem. Trim the seam allowance close to the stitching.

2. Slide the stem cover onto the stem, and glue it closed at both ends.

Put the Flower Together

1. Beginning with a small petal, cut a small slit into the end of the petal and insert one end of the stem into the slit. Glue it in place.

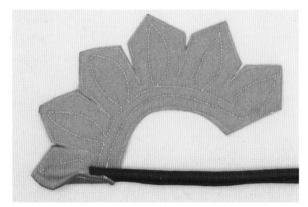

Insert stem in slit.

2. Begin wrapping the other small petals in a circular pattern down the stem, overlapping the previous petals and gluing them into place. Continue with the larger petals until all the petals are glued onto the stem.

3. To attach the leaf, apply glue in a triangle along the lower edge of the leaf. Wrap the glued edges of the leaf around the stem below the flower so that about 3″ of stem is visible between the flower and the leaf.

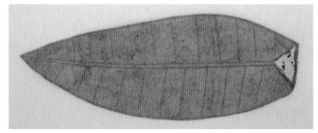

Apply glue.

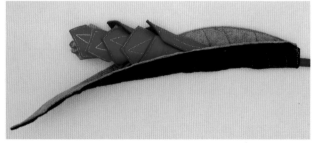

Attach leaf.

4. Use the photograph of the finished flowers as a guide to shape and arrange the petals and leaves to simulate authentic blooms.

These aptly named flowers, with their brilliant colors and shapes and lush foliage, create the perfect focal point for casual or contemporary decor. They make a stunning display when used alone, or you can combine them with other exotic blooms such as Ginger and Anthurium for a truly tropical extravaganza.

Bird of Paradise

materials

See pages 6–7 for basic supplies.

FOR EACH FLOWER YOU WILL NEED:

YELLOW FELT: 1 piece 4″ × 8″ for the stamens

ORANGE FELT: 1 piece 4″ × 8″ for the stamens

BLUE FELT: 1 piece 3″ × 5″ for the small petal

PURPLE FELT: 1 piece 3″ × 5″ for the small petal

VIOLET FELT: 1 piece 5″ × 8″ for the outer large petal

BASIL GREEN FELT: 1 piece 5″ × 8″ for the outer large petal; 1 strip, 1¹/₂″ × 25″ for the flower stem cover; 1 strip, 1¹/₂″ × 17″ for the leaf stem cover; 1 piece 6″ × 11″ for the leaf

FOREST GREEN FELT: 1 piece 6″ × 11″ for the leaf

¹/₄″-DIAMETER STEM: 1 piece 24″ long for the flower; 1 piece 15″ long for the leaf

18-GAUGE COVERED FLORIST WIRE: 7 pieces, each 6″ long, for the stamens and the petals; 1 piece 10″ long for the leaf

FLORIST TAPE

instructions

See pages 8–11 for basic techniques.

Make the Petals and Leaves

1. Make templates for the Bird of Paradise small and outer large petals, stamen, and leaf using the patterns on the pullout.

2. Trace the stamen template 5 times onto yellow felt. Transfer the topstitching lines. Layer this marked felt with a piece of orange felt.

3. Trace the small petal template once onto blue felt. Transfer the topstitching lines. Layer this marked felt with a piece of purple felt.

4. Trace the outer large petal template once onto basil green felt. Transfer the topstitching lines. Layer this marked felt with a piece of orange felt.

5. Trace the leaf template once onto forest green felt. Transfer the topstitching lines. Layer this marked felt with a piece of basil green felt.

6. **Before cutting out each piece,** stitch carefully around the outlines using coordinating thread for the leaves and contrasting thread for the petals. Topstitch as indicated to create surface texture on the flower petals and veins on the leaves. When topstitching, be sure to leave the center channels open at the bases of the leaves and small petal for inserting wire.

7. Cut out each piece slightly beyond the outline stitching.

Stitch leaves and petals, then cut out.

8. Insert florist wire into the yellow/orange stamens and through the channel in the purple/blue petal. For the outer petal, cut a 2″ slit in the center of the channel at the wide end of the petal, then insert the wire through the remaining stitched channel. Trim the wire close to the end of the slit.

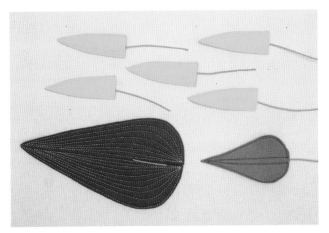

Insert wires.

9. Place a dab of glue in the center of each stamen to hold the wire in place and then pinch together the lower edges of each stamen and small petal. Glue the edges to secure them.

Pinch and glue lower edges.

10. Grasp the wires extending from the stamens and small petals and twist them together with pliers. Place the wires next to the end of the 24″ stem and wrap them and the stem with florist tape.

Twist wires together.

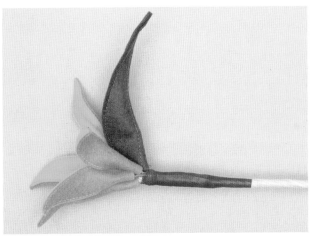

Align with stem and cover with florist tape.

Make the Stems

1. Fold each stem cover in half lengthwise. Measure and stitch them to create a snug fit for the stems. Trim the seam allowances close to the stitching.

2. Slide the stem covers onto the stems. Glue the flower stem cover in place at the base of the flower, covering the point at which the flower meets the stem.

Glue stem cover in place.

3. To finish the lower end of the flower stem and both ends of the leaf stem, trim away the excess fabric and glue the edges closed over the stem.

4. Attach the leaf to the leaf stem by applying glue to the lower edge of the leaf and wrapping it around the stem at the top.

Put the Flower Together

1. Place a dab of glue in the center of the slit of the violet side of the outer petal. Attach it by folding it around the cluster of stamens. Fold and glue one side. Then overlap the other edge to create a scoop-shaped flower.

Fold and glue one side.

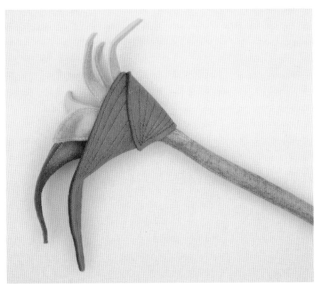

Overlap other edge.

2. Let the glue dry completely, then shape the flower by straightening the stamens vertically and bending the florist wire in the blue/purple petal so that it is positioned horizontally.

3. Use the photograph of the finished flowers (page 63) as a guide to shape and arrange the petals and leaves to simulate authentic blooms.

The bold color and shape of these island favorites will add a splash of bright color to any room. You can create a sleek, dramatic arrangement with a few simple blooms, or fill a tall vase with the graceful heart-shaped leaves and blossoms for an opulent display.

anthurium

materials

See pages 6–7 for basic supplies.

FOR EACH FLOWER YOU WILL NEED:

RED FELT: 2 pieces, each 6″ × 6″, for the flower

BRIGHT YELLOW FELT: 2 pieces, each 1″ × 3″, for the stamen

LEAF GREEN FELT: 1 piece 6″ × 8″ for the leaves

FOREST GREEN FELT: 1 piece 6″ × 8″ for the leaves; 1 strip 1¹/₂″ × 26″ for the flower stem cover; 1 strip 1¹/₂″ × 26″ for the leaf stem cover

¹/₄″-DIAMETER STEM: 1 piece 24″ long for the flower; 1 piece 24″ long for the leaf

18-GAUGE COVERED FLORIST WIRE: 1 piece 8″ long for the leaf; 1 piece 5″ long for the stamen

instructions

See pages 8–11 for basic techniques.

Make the Petals and Leaves

1. Make templates for the Anthurium flower, stamen, and leaf using the patterns on the pullout.

2. Trace the flower template once onto red felt. Transfer the topstitching lines. Layer this marked felt with another piece of red felt.

3. Trace the stamen template once onto yellow felt. Layer this marked felt with another piece of yellow felt.

4. Trace the leaf template once onto forest green felt. Transfer the topstitching lines. Layer this marked felt with a piece of leaf green felt.

5. **Before cutting out each piece,** stitch carefully around the outlines using coordinating thread for the stamen and contrasting thread for the flower and leaf. Topstitch as indicated to create the leaf veins and surface texture on the flower. Leave an opening where indicated on the leaf and stamen patterns. Cut out each piece slightly beyond the outline stitching.

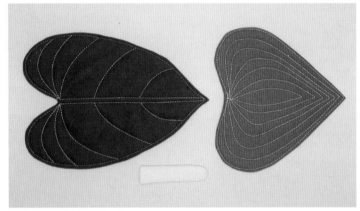

Stitch petal, leaf, and stamen, then cut out.

Make the Stamen, Leaf, and Stems

1. Cut a $^1/_2$″ × 2″ rectangle from the stamen scraps and glue it around the end of a piece of covered florist wire to create a padded stamen base. Slide the stamen cover onto the padded stem end and glue it in place.

Padded stamen base

Slide on stamen cover.

2. Fold each stem cover in half lengthwise. Measure and stitch it to create a snug fit for the stem. Trim the seam allowance close to the stitching.

3. Align the wire from the stamen with one stem and glue them together. Slide a stem cover onto the flower stem and glue it in place at the point at which the stamen meets the stem.

4. Insert the 8″ covered florist wire through the channel in the leaf and glue it to secure it, leaving about 1″ extending from the stem end of the leaf.

5. Glue the wire extending from the leaf onto the other stem. Slide a stem cover onto the leaf stem. Glue carefully at the point on the underside of the leaf where the leaf and the stem meet.

Glue cover to underside of leaf.

6. To finish the lower stem ends, trim away the excess fabric and glue the edges closed.

Put the Flower Together

1. Place a dab of glue in the center of the curved edge of the flower. Attach it to the stamen, pinching the lower edges of the flower together around the stamen. Let the glue dry completely, then fold back the flower so that it is almost perpendicular to the stem and stamen.

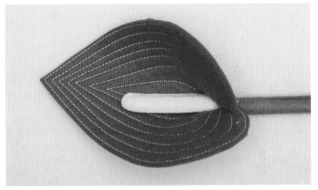

Glue lower edges of flower around stamen.

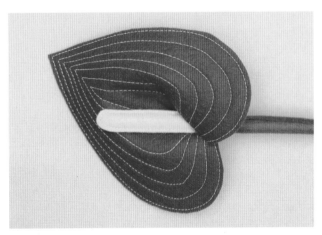

Shape flower.

2. Use the photograph of the finished flowers (page 67) as a guide to shape and arrange the petals and leaves to simulate authentic blooms.

The bold scale of this exotic flower makes it an excellent choice for stand-alone trop-ical drama. The bright red fleshy flowers banded by yellow and green overlap one another as they cascade down the serpentine stalk. Delicate feathery stamens peek out from beneath the showy flowers to add textural contrast. Lush oversized leaves surround the stalk, forming the perfect backdrop for this showy specimen.

Heliconia
(Crab Claw)

materials

See pages 6–7 for basic supplies.

FOR THE FLOWER AND LEAVES AS SHOWN, YOU WILL NEED:

RED FELT: 1 piece 8″ × 26″ for the inner petals

YELLOW FELT: 1 piece 8″ × 26″ for the outer petals

BRIGHT GREEN FELT: 1 piece 8″ × 6″ for the flower centers

FOREST GREEN FELT: 1 piece 24″ × 32″ for the large leaves; 1 piece 14″ × 21″ for the small leaves

BASIL GREEN FELT: 1 piece 24″ × 32″ for the large leaves; 1 piece 14″ × 21″ for the small leaves

WINE FELT: 2 strips, each 1¹/₂″ × 32″, for the stick stem covers

BROWN FELT: 6 strips, each 1¹/₂″ × 32″, for the flower and the leaf stem covers

¹/₄″-DIAMETER STEM: 8 pieces, each 30″ long, for the flower, the sticks, and the leaves

1″-DIAMETER STEM: 1 piece 24″ long for the stalk

18-GAUGE FLORIST WIRE: 6 pieces, each 7″ long, for the flower centers; 5 pieces, each 22″ long, for the leaves

YELLOW RATTAIL CORD: 1 yard for stamens

GREEN RATTAIL CORD: 1 yard for stamens

FLORIST TAPE

instructions

See pages 8–11 for basic techniques.

Make the Petals

1. Make templates for the Heliconia inner and outer petals, flower center, and small and large leaves using the patterns on the pullout.

2. Trace the templates for the outer petal 6 times onto yellow felt, the inner petal 6 times onto red felt, and the flower center 6 times onto bright green felt. Transfer the topstitching lines.

3. Carefully cut out all the yellow petals, red petals, and bright green flower centers. Arrange the layers in place on the yellow petals.

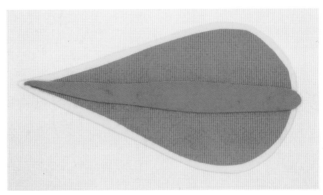

Arrange layers on yellow petals.

4. Stitch close to the edges of the green flower centers using yellow thread to create wire channels. Be careful to leave an opening at the widest end of each petal for inserting the florist wire. Stitch along the outer edges of the red layer and topstitch in a concentric pattern to create an allover texture.

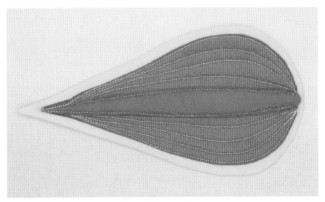

Stitch along edges of layers, then add topstitching.

5. Insert a 7″ piece of wire in the pocket created by the flower center.

Make the Stamens

1. Cut the rattail cord into 6″ lengths. Grasp one end of the rattail, and pull on the white thread cord that is woven through the center. The outer satin threads will release and form a small pouf. The white cord will make a small curly center. Repeat at the other end of the rattail. Fold pairs of yellow and green rattail pieces in half.

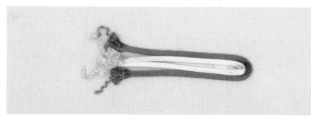

Make rattail cord stamen.

2. Glue a pair of rattail stamens onto the back of each yellow layer, leaving the pouf free to extend below the flower when complete.

Glue stamen to inside layer of flower.

Make the Leaves

1. Trace the large leaf template 4 times and the small leaf template 3 times onto forest green felt. Mark the topstitching lines on all the leaves. Layer this marked felt with a piece of basil green felt.

2. Before cutting out the leaves, stitch the outlines with contrasting thread, leaving the lower edges open as indicated. Then stitch the channel for the wire through the center of each leaf. Continue topstitching all the lines as indicated, creating an allover pattern on the leaves. Cut out the leaves slightly beyond the outline stitching.

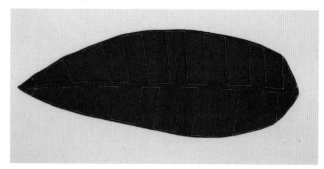

Stitch leaves, then cut out.

Make the Stems

1. Fold the wine felt stem covers in half lengthwise. Measure and stitch them to create a snug fit for 2 of the ¼″ stems. Trim the seam allowances close to the stitching.

2. Slide the stem covers onto 2 stems, and glue them neatly closed at both ends. Set those stems aside.

3. Fold 1 brown stem cover in half lengthwise. Measure, mark, and stitch it to create a snug fit for another ¼″ stem. Trim away the seam allowance slightly beyond the stitching.

4. Slide this brown stem cover onto a ¼″ stem and glue it closed at both ends. Bend one end of the brown-covered stem so that it forms a serpentine shape with 12″ of straight stem at one end. This will be the main flower stem.

5. Fold the remaining brown stem covers in half lengthwise. Measure, mark, and stitch them to create a snug fit for the remaining ¼″ stems. Trim away the seam allowances slightly beyond the stitching. You will use various lengths of these stem covers for the leaf stems.

Put the Plant Together

1. Begin at the bent end of the serpentine stem. Fold and glue one flower in half lengthwise over the end of the stem, so the widest point of the folded flower encases the end of the stem and the stamens extend from the folded flower as shown.

Glue petals in place.

2. Following the serpentine curves, fold and glue another flower onto the opposite side, overlapping the previous flower, so that the flower forms an angle with the previous one. Continue alternating sides until all the flowers have been glued onto the stem. Use clips or clothespins to hold the flowers in place while the hot glue cools and hardens.

Use clips to hold petals in place.

3. Arrange the 2 wine stems on either side of the flower stem and the 1˝ stalk stem. Tape them together at the base of the flower stem with florist tape. The stalk stem is for support only and will not show when the flower is complete.

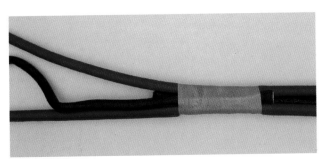

Tape stems together at base of flower stem.

4. Wrap a large leaf around the taped stems so that the point of the leaf extends well above the taped area, and glue it firmly in place. Allow it to cool completely before proceeding to the second leaf, which will wrap around the previous leaf and stems from the other side.

Wrap leaves around stem base and glue in place.

5. Insert floral wire into the remaining 5 leaves, allowing the wire to extend approximately 6˝ beyond the length of the leaf.

6. Align each leaf wire with a stem and glue it in place. Cut the stems to varying lengths. Slide stem covers over these stems. Glue them in place where the stem cover meets each leaf. Trim and glue the other end of the stem cover neatly closed.

Attach stems and covers to leaves.

7. Use the photograph of the finished flowers (page 70) as a guide to shape and arrange the petals and leaves to simulate authentic blooms.

Live Orchids are so unusual by their nature that they sometimes don't look like they could possibly be real. However, this blooming exotic rivals the real thing with its intricately sculpted center, fleshy petals and leaves, and luscious color combinations. You'll find that despite these attributes, the blooming Orchid plants are relatively quick and easy to make. They're a great way to impress your friends with your newly found botanical skills and they'll lend an air of upscale sophistication to your decor.

Orchid Plant

materials

See pages 6–7 for basic supplies.

TO MAKE THE PLANT AS SHOWN, YOU WILL NEED:

VIOLET FELT: 1 piece 5″ × 5″ for the flower center

PUMPKIN FELT: 1 piece 5″ × 5″ for the flower center

LIGHT VIOLET FELT: 2 pieces, each 7″ × 10″ for the petals

LEAF GREEN FELT: 1 piece 20″ × 22″ for the leaves

FOREST GREEN FELT: 1 piece 20″ × 22″ for the leaves; 1 strip 1¹/₂″ × 17″ for the stem cover

¹/₄″-DIAMETER STEM: 1 piece 15″ long

18-GAUGE COVERED FLORIST WIRE: 2 pieces, each 6″ long, for the petals; 1 piece 9″ long for the small leaf; 5 pieces, each 13″ long, for the triple petal, the flower center, and the medium leaves; 4 pieces, each 15″ long, for the large leaves

FLORIST TAPE

instructions

See pages 8–11 for basic techniques.

Make the Petals

1. Make templates for the Orchid double and triple petals; the flower center; and the small, medium, and large Orchid leaves using the patterns on the pullout.

2. Trace the flower center template once onto violet felt. Transfer the top-stitching lines. Layer this marked felt with a piece of pumpkin felt.

3. Trace the double and triple Orchid petals once each onto light violet felt. Transfer the topstitching lines. Layer this marked felt with another piece of light violet felt.

4. Trace the small leaf template once, the medium leaf template 3 times, and the large leaf template 4 times onto leaf green felt. Transfer the topstitching lines. Layer this marked felt with a piece of forest green felt.

5. **Before cutting out the Orchid center,** stitch carefully around the outline, using contrasting thread, and topstitch as indicated to create surface texture and the channel through the center for inserting the wire.

6. Cut out the flower center slightly beyond the stitching, carefully clipping at points and curves to avoid cutting into the stitching.

Stitch flower center, then cut out.

7. Fold the flower center in half lengthwise with the pumpkin side in, and stitch diagonally through both layers from the center to the edge where indicated by the dotted line on the pattern.

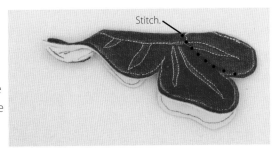

Fold and stitch through both layers.

8. Fold the pointed ends together with the violet sides in, and stitch through the center of the points where indicated by the dotted line on the pattern.

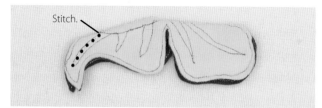

Stitch through center of points.

9. Flip and turn to open out the flower center so that the sewn tube extends from the center front. Cut a small hole at the center back of the pumpkin side to insert the covered florist wire into the topstitched channel. Glue it in place at the hole.

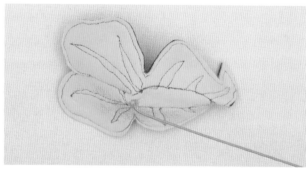

Open flower center and insert wire.

10. **Before cutting out the double petal,** stitch carefully around the outlines, using coordinating thread, and topstitch to create the veins and the channels for the wire. Cut the petals out slightly beyond the outline stitching. Cut 2 small holes near the center of the back. Fold a 6″ piece of wire and the petals in half, with right sides facing. Insert the wire into the holes and slide it into the channels. Open the petals out flat.

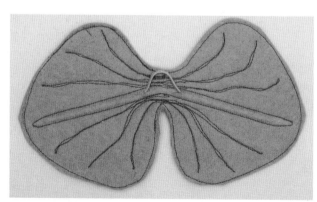

Insert wire into double-petal channels.

11. To make the triple petal, repeat the same process as above in Step 10 to insert a 6″ piece of wire into 2 petals, then insert an additional 12″ piece of wire into the third petal, leaving the end extending from the back of the flower.

Leave wire extending from flower back.

Make the Leaves

1. **Before cutting out the leaves,** stitch carefully around the outlines, using coordinating thread, and topstitch to create texture and a channel through the center of each leaf for inserting the wire.

2. Cut out each leaf slightly beyond the stitching and insert a piece of florist wire into the channel, leaving at least 6″ of wire extending beyond the bottom of each leaf.

Stitch leaves, then cut out and insert wire.

Make the Stem

1. Fold the stem cover in half lengthwise. Measure and stitch it to create a snug fit for the stem. Trim the seam allowance close to the stitching.

2. Slide the stem cover onto the stem, and glue it closed at one end.

Put the Plant Together

1. Thread the wire extending from the flower center through the wire loop on the back of the double petals and pull it snugly together, with the front side of the petals touching the back of the flower center. Glue the petals together invisibly between the layers.

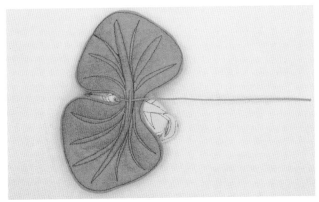

Thread flower center wire through double petal's wire loop.

Glue petals to back of flower center.

2. Cut a small hole at the center of the triple-petal section and thread the wire from the flower center / double-petal section through the hole. Pull together the 3 layers and twist the wires together on the back side of the triple-petal section. Glue together the petals invisibly between the layers.

Thread wire through triple-petal hole.

Glue petals / flower center to triple petals.

3. To attach the flower to the stem, slide the stem cover back slightly from the loose end, and align the wires next to the stem. Secure it by wrapping the stem and wires with florist tape. Slide the stem cover over the stem end, open the seam slightly at the end of the stem cover, and glue the cover carefully to the back of the flower where the stem and flower come together.

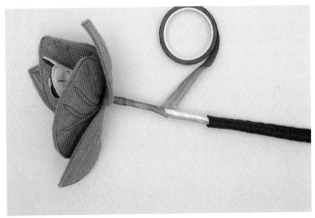

Align wires with stem and secure with florist tape.

Glue stem cover to back of flower.

4. To attach the leaves to one another, begin with the small leaf and apply glue in a triangle along the lower edge of the leaf. Fold the leaf in half with the lightest side in, and hold it snugly in place until the glue is dry. You can use a clip or a clothespin to hold it while you wait for the glue to dry.

5. Continue attaching medium leaves one at a time using the same method. The leaves should be glued on opposite sides of the plant so that the lower ends overlap slightly.

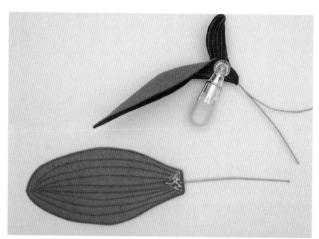

Fold and glue medium leaves.

6. Once the medium leaves are attached, arrange the flower stem next to the leaves so that about 6″ of stem extends below the leaves. Wrap the exposed wires from the leaves around the lower end of the flower stem and glue the bases of the leaves to the stem to secure them.

Attach flower stem.

7. Attach the large leaves one at a time using the same method. The leaves should be glued on opposite sides of the plant so that the lower ends overlap slightly.

Glue large leaves in place.

8. Use the photograph of the finished flowers (page 74) as a guide to shape and arrange the petals and leaves to simulate authentic blooms.

Photo by Sonny Knox

About the Author

Lynne Farris brings a lifetime of experience in fabric arts to the world of crafts and do-it-yourself home decor. Her designs are often featured in leading craft magazines, and she is a frequent guest on HGTV. She works as a creative consultant to several leading manufacturers and is the owner of Lynne Farris Gallery in Atlanta, Georgia, where many of her textile works are on display. To learn more about Lynne, visit her website at www.lynnefarrisdesigns.com.

Also by Lynne Farris

Resources

LYNNE FARRIS DESIGNS
1101 Juniper Street #404
Atlanta GA 30309
Stems, materials, kits, fringe, and other supplies for felt flowers
Email: lynnefarris@lynnefarrisdesigns.com
Website: www.lynnefarrisdesigns.com

NATIONAL NONWOVENS
Wool felt (wholesale only)
Website: www.nationalnonwovens.com

C&T PUBLISHING
Stems for felt flowers
Website: www.ctpub.com

FOR A LIST OF OTHER FINE BOOKS FROM C&T PUBLISHING, ASK FOR A FREE CATALOG:
C&T Publishing, Inc.
P.O. Box 1456
Lafayette, CA 94549
(800) 284-1114
Email: ctinfo@ctpub.com
Website: www.ctpub.com

FOR SEWING AND QUILTING SUPPLIES:
Cotton Patch Mail Order
3405 Hall Lane, Dept. CTB
Lafayette, CA 94549
(800) 835-4418
(925) 283-7883
Email: quiltusa@yahoo.com
Website: www.quiltusa.com

great titles

from C&T PUBLISHING

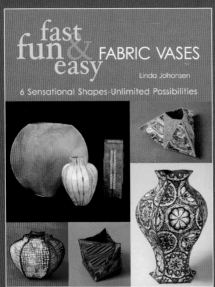
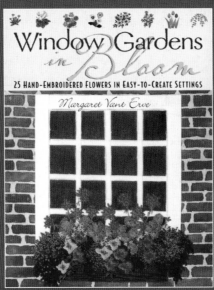

Available at your local retailer or
www.ctpub.com or 800.284.1114